THE BLACK ATHLETE

A Shameful Story

THE BLACK ATHLETE

A Shameful Story

THE MYTH OF INTEGRATION IN AMERICAN SPORT
BY JACK OLSEN

TIME-LIFE BOOKS, NEW YORK

Other books by Jack Olsen

THE MAD WORLD OF BRIDGE
OVER THE FENCE IS OUT (as Jonathan Rhoades)
THE CLIMB UP TO HELL
BRIDGE IS MY GAME (with Charles Goren)
BLACK IS BEST—*The Riddle of Cassius Clay*
SILENCE ON MONTE SOLE

CONTENTS

"It Was Profitable Both Ways": The Anatomy of a Cruel Delusion

1

Every morning the world of sports wakes up and congratulates itself on its contributions to race relations. The litany has been repeated so often that it is believed almost universally. It goes: "Look what sports has done for the Negro."

To be sure, there are a few men—and they think of themselves as fair-minded—who are willing to suggest that perhaps the Negro has done something for sports in return. Says George McCarty, athletic director of the University of Texas at El Paso, "In general, the nigger athlete is a little hungrier, and we have been blessed with having some real outstanding ones. We think they've done a lot for us, and we think we've done a lot for them."

The McCarty attitude is echoed on many campuses. Says a university president: "Sure, the Negroes helped our image, but don't forget, they got built up too. Every one of them that's been here got out of the ghetto. Four of our colored alumni are playing pro basketball right now, and seven are in pro football, and you can't just say that we got a bunch of cattle in here and milked them. It was profitable both ways."

Some argue that anyone with two eyes can see what sports has done for the Negro, and offer Willie Mays as Exhibit A. Where would Willie be without baseball? Chopping cotton? Firing a smelter in Birmingham? Or take Bill Russell, player-coach of the Boston Celtics. He goes around making antiwhite remarks, but they

7

still give him a six-figure check for playing basketball. Without sports, the argument runs, he would be lucky to be working as a janitor in his hometown of Oakland. Jim Brown is another one. He retires from pro football with a fortune in his sock and becomes an overnight success as a movie actor, all because of sports, and then founds an organization aimed at getting black men jobs, all the while talking out of the side of his mouth about the whites. Why, sports *created* Jim Brown, the apologists crow; sports gave him a free education at Syracuse University and then catapulted him to national fame as a star fullback for the Cleveland Browns.

That's the way the argument goes, and ultimately it reaches the classic in case histories: a six-foot-eight-inch 250-pound assistant professor of sociology who wears love beads and shades and a black beret, and urges Negro athletes to boycott the Olympics, rise up against the athletic departments of various colleges and smite the white sports establishment with all their collective power. This fanatical superblack is Harry Edwards, who came out of East St. Louis, Illinois, where he attended various jails as a youth before it was discovered that he could whirl a discus half a mile and San Jose State College offered him an athletic scholarship.

Thus one reaches the ultimate irony—Harry Edwards, considered by some to be the mouthpiece of the black athletic rebellion, himself was lifted out of the ghetto by the white sports establishment. Why, if it were not for sports, Harry Edwards probably would be alongside his brother Donald, serving 25 years to life in the Iowa State Penitentiary for armed robbery, or following in the footsteps of his father, an alumnus of Pontiac State Penitentiary, or his mother, who once came home from a street brawl wearing 86 stitches.

You can hear these arguments any night of the week in the saloon of your choice, even in the *Negro* saloon of your choice. The cliché that sports has been good to the Negro has been accepted by black and white, liberal and conservative, intellectual and red-neck. And the Negro athlete who has the nerve to suggest that all is not perfect is branded as ungrateful, a cur that bites the hand. "If only we could achieve in housing, in education, in economic opportunity, all the things we have achieved in sports," says a typically grateful Negro leader, "the race problem in the United States would disappear."

However, the Negro athletes do not agree. Almost to a man, they are dissatisfied, disgruntled and disillusioned.

Black professional athletes say they are underpaid, shunted into certain stereotyped positions and treated like subhumans by Paleolithic coaches who regard them as watermelon-eating idiots.

Black collegiate athletes say they are dehumanized, exploited and discarded, and some even say they were happier back in the ghetto.

A member of the University of Houston's coaching staff once made the mistake of telling halfback Warren McVea, "I think this university's athletic program has been pretty damned good to you." Warren McVea, a short, black artillery shell of a man, snapped back: "I think I've been pretty damned good to this university. I want you to remember one thing: you came to me, I didn't come to you."

"People say, 'Wasn't football good to you?' " recalls Jim Parker, retired All-Pro lineman of the Baltimore

Colts. "I say, 'Hell, no, I've been good to it.' Football did no better for me than what I put into it."

Someone asked Percy Harris, football line coach at all-black Du Sable High School in Chicago, what he got out of four years of scholarship athletics at various institutions of higher learning in the Southwest. "Well, let's see," Harris mused. "At the University of New Mexico I got a sweater. At Cameron State College in Oklahoma I got a blanket. At Southwestern State I got a jacket and a blanket."

"Black students aren't given athletic scholarships for the purpose of education," says Harry Edwards. "Blacks are brought in to perform. Any education they get is incidental to their main job, which is playing sports. In most cases, their college lives are educational blanks." With rare exceptions, the American college coach expects his Negro athletes to concentrate on the job for which they were hired. The aim is neither graduation nor education. The *sine qua non* for the Negro athlete is maintaining his eligibility.

"There is nothing in the world so forlorn and useless as a Negro college athlete who has used up his eligibility," says a white sociologist who, incidentally, functions as a lineman in the National Football League. "If he's going into the pros, of course, that's something different. But how many of them will make it to the pros—one in a hundred?"

At the end of the last second of the last minute of the last hour of a Negro athlete's eligibility, he is likely to find himself dumped unceremoniously into the harsh academic world. Tutors who wrote his themes disappear; professors who gave him superior grades for inferior work stiffen their marking standards overnight; counselors who advised courses in basket weaving and fly casting suddenly begin pointing out that certain postponed courses in English and mathematics and history must be passed before graduation.

Thus the mirage of a college degree continues to fade in the distance, and that brings up the second fundamental fact about the Negro athletes in American colleges; they rarely graduate with their classes, and the majority of them do not graduate at all. They are wet-nursed in their courses long enough to remain eligible, and after all the shortcuts and duplicity and outright cheating, they return to the Negro community as "leaders" and "college men" when in fact they have done little more than hire out as Hessians for four years, or long enough to bring a conference championship to Old Siwash. Yet their fame is such in the black community that Negro children are eager to follow the same futile course.

The example of the black professional athlete has a similar effect in the community. He shows small boys the way. Sports becomes a bridge out of the ghetto. But as the football-playing sociologist observes, "For how many? Who has sports led out of the ghetto? Bobby Mitchell? Yes. Jim Brown? Yes. Sam Jones? Yes, and Richie Allen, Willie Mays, Curt Flood. Some would say the list is endless, but that's the hell of it—it isn't. It's really terribly finite." At the most, sports has led a few thousand Negroes out of the ghetto. But for hundreds of thousands of other Negroes it has substituted a meaningless dream. It has helped to perpetuate an oppressive system. For every Willie Mays or Bob Hayes, there are countless Negroes who sacrificed their childhood to baseball gloves and shoulder pads. They could not see another way out. Among these are the Negro doctors who never were and the desperately needed Negro lawyers and city planners. This has been the major effect of sports on the Negro, and it overrides all others.

James Baldwin, black author of *The Fire Next Time*, has written: "Every Negro boy . . . realizes, at once, profoundly, because he wants to live, that he stands in great peril and must find, with speed, a 'thing,' a gimmick, to lift him out, to start him on his way. *And it does not matter what the gimmick is.*" For some it is narcotics. For others it is crime. For more than a few, the only gimmick that seems feasible and safe is sports.

Says Harry Gunner, star defensive end for Oregon State who signed a professional football contract with the Cincinnati Bengals, "When I was a little kid in Port Arthur, Texas, I thought I wanted to be a doctor. But that went through the window when television came in and I started watching sports."

"Boys like that are totally wrapped up in being the athlete," says Professor Charles G. Hurst of Howard University. "Sure, Wilt Chamberlain makes two hundred and fifty thousand dollars, and Bob Gibson makes eighty thousand to a hundred thousand dollars a year. But in reality how many can? The Negro needs to know that there are alternatives available other than athletics. There is nothing less wanted in our society than a worn-out Negro athlete. If these boys don't make it as professionals—and what percentage does?—the system has not prepared them to engage in any other avenue of economic endeavor on a competitive basis."

To Melvin Rogers, gym teacher and basketball coach at all-Negro Eula D. Britton High School, in Rayville, Louisiana, the problem is part of his daily life. "If people only knew what we have to go through, to produce that one boy out of a hundred who makes it. People say, 'My, my, aren't you proud? You coached Elvin Hayes, and now he's got a four-hundred-and-forty-thousand-dollar contract in pro basketball.' Well, I'm proud of Elvin, sure I am, but look out that window over there. See that big fellow playing baseball? He went to school here, had a high I.Q. too, but for him it was sports or nothing. He was a catcher; he could throw from his knees to second base when he was a sophomore in high school. He was right out there on that field morning and night. Baseball, baseball, baseball. He got into college, but he didn't have the basics. He hadn't paid enough attention in school to anything but baseball. He couldn't diagram a sentence or talk about Othello. All he knew how to do was hang onto the third strike. He went up to the majors for a tryout and didn't make it, and now you can see him around here, working out with the boys on the diamond. Age caught up with him, and he's a nothing. He fell for a dream. He could have been just about anything he wanted—except a major-league catcher."

The Negro who overemphasizes sports has become a tragic caricature of his race. One sees him circling the high-school track long after the others have gone home, or practicing lay-ups on the playground court until it is too dark to see if the shots go in. "A white boy will play if he doesn't have to practice too long," says Will Robinson, tennis and basketball coach at Pershing High School in Detroit, a man who has steered some 150 Negro athletes toward college on athletic scholarships. "The white boy has other things he would rather do. People keep reminding me that there is a difference in physical ability between the races, but I think there isn't. The Negro boy just practices longer and harder. The Negro has the keener desire to excel in sports because it is more mandatory for his future opportunities than it is for a white boy. There are nine thousand different jobs available to a person if he is white."

The Negro who chases the brass ring of sports to the exclusion of other aspects of his life does so because he wants to feel alive. Says Harry Edwards: "Because the black kid is in a deprived situation, he can't go and jump in the swimming pool, he can't get on his bicycle and ride across town, or go to the mountains skiing. So instead he gets him a peach basket and nails it up, or he gets him a doll's head and a broomstick and begins to play baseball, or he begins to run up and down the street because there's nothing else to do. He creates games. It is like the study that was done in California. They got fifteen black youngsters and said, 'Okay, I want you to take this wall and make up as many games as you possibly can using nothing but this ball.' Then they went and got fifteen white youngsters and did the same thing on the opposite wall from the blacks. The black kids came up with a hundred and fifteen games. The white kids came up with nine. Nine games and they're exhausted! And when the time ran out, the black kids were still making up games."

In this way, the Negro develops a feeling for sports and turns it into a system of esthetics, his own private art. Sport becomes a *raison d'être*, and perforce the Negro athlete becomes more skilled than the white. "Black people are playing in mud and rain and snow and everything else," Harry Edwards says, "and from the time that they are able to dribble a basketball they are out

14

jumping and shooting and running. Crackers don't do this. They ride bicycles. There is a difference in ability, but this doesn't necessarily mean that this is an innate physical difference, indigenous to the races. It is a matter of cultural environment, cultural development."

If the Negro who is "out jumping and shooting and running" fails to become a Wilt Chamberlain or an Elgin Baylor or an Oscar Robertson, he becomes Professor Hurst's "worn-out Negro athlete," competing for employment in an economic market that has little use for the breakaway dribble and the fadeaway jump. Elvin Hayes' former coach puts it another way. "A white kid tries to become President of the United States," says Melvin Rogers, "and all the skills and knowledge he picks up on the way can be used in a thousand different jobs. A black kid tries to become Willie Mays, and all the tools he picks up on the way are useless to him if he doesn't become Willie Mays."

Even if he has nothing to worry about in terms of talent, the Negro high-school athlete risks running into a variety of problems off the field when he gets to college. Most often, he picks up his college scholarship and enters a schizophrenic world where he is lionized on the field and ignored off it. "I don't want to be known as the fastest nigger on campus," says Tommy Smith of San Jose State College, but he is. Most star Negro athletes try to become accustomed to this double standard, but few succeed. A black pole-vaulter listened to thousands cheer as he performed in Madison Square Garden, but when he dressed and tried to make his way through the crowds outside on Eighth Avenue, he heard, "Hey, boy, watch where you're sticking that goddam pole!" The meet was over; he was a nigger again. **15**

Other black athletes twist and squirm and fight to become accepted, suffer losses, lick their wounds and return to fight again, and more often than not they wind up embittered and discouraged.

Don Shanklin, star running back of the University of Kansas, is one of these resisters, and although he has scored a few minor social victories on the campus, his college career has been a shatteringly disillusioning experience. Shanklin has steadfastly refused to accept an inferior position in the university's social structure, but the inferior position has steadfastly been thrust upon him. Now he is coldly cynical. During most of his years at KU he wanted nothing more than to depart from the lovely green campus in the hills of Lawrence as fast as he could get away.

What does Don Shanklin's college career add up to? "Well, it kept me off the trash trucks in Amarillo," he says. "That's where most of the cats in my hometown wind up." He has learned next to nothing. All he was really permitted to do at KU was make some long runs with a football. All he added to his own experience was four years of acute loneliness and alienation in the white man's world—and a chance for a pro contract. He is honest and direct and admits that the contract is what he was really after. And the alumni and the other sports fanatics around the campus seem satisfied by this state of affairs. You can hear them practically any time of the day or night around the Jayhawk Cafe or the lounge of the plush lily-white Beta house or the locker-room of the Lawrence Country Club, telling one another what a lucky guy Don Shanklin is, and how lucky KU was to get him. They are telling one another what sports has done for the Negro.

16

In return for what he was supposed to be getting out of sports, the Negro athlete was expected, until very recently, to stand fast and take it, keep his mouth shut, and perform valiantly in front of cheering white audiences. Regardless of whether he was professional or amateur, if he wanted respect off the field, if he wanted to collect the hero worship and social advantages that are the traditional reward of the star athlete, he had to go to Blacktown. Long into the night, he would hold court around a restaurant kitchen steam table in Harlem or Roxbury or Hough or Watts, while one by one people of his own color dropped by and congratulated him on the third-round knockout or the home run he hit in the 11th to win the game. Each such achievement was regarded as an achievement for the Negro race. The totality of such achievements was going to add up to full equality at some vague future date. Meanwhile the Negro athletes were demigods in the Negro community and jigaboos in the white. And their essential roles were recessive. They merely endured. Professor Sterling A. Brown of Howard University wrote a poem about Jack Johnson, the first Negro heavyweight champion:

One thing you left with us, Jack Johnson.
One thing before they got you.

You used to stand there like a man,
Taking punishment
With a golden, spacious grin;
Confident.
Inviting big Jim Jeffries, who was boring in:
"Heah ah is, big boy; yuh sees whah Ise at.
Come on in. . . ."

Thanks, Jack, for that.

By permission of Sterling A. Brown, from *Southern Road*, Harcourt, Brace (and World), 1932.

No disrespect intended for Dr. Brown, a leading American Negro poet and educator, but the era of Jack Johnson and his mild-mannered successors, good men like Joe Louis, Roy Campanella and Willie Mays, is long ended. White reporters, realizing Louis' vast popularity among Negroes, used to write deep-think columns explaining Joe's popularity in terms of his modesty, his self-effacement, his dignity and a dozen other qualities that made him a "credit to his race." Joe had these qualities, to be sure, and they recommended him to whites, but they were not what attracted the black fans. Negroes loved Joe Louis for one reason: he was knocking white men on their tails, getting away with it, *getting paid for it.* Sterling Stuckey, a Negro who has taught history at the University of Illinois, says:

"All along, the black athlete like Joe Louis has meant something to black middle-class people that is quite different from what athletes mean to the society at large. The black athlete is like the black poet in that he is able to do something—in this case on the field—that the Negro is not able to do off the field, or in life in general." The old-style black athlete, within the narrow confines of the sports setting, could meet the white man on his own terms and demonstrate his worth. "Black people equated an athletic triumph with triumph over whites who have kept them oppressed for centuries," Stuckey says. "Fighters like Jack Johnson and Joe Louis were carrying sixteen million black people into the ring with them. Sports was an arena in which black people could act out their aggressions against white people."

And behind every victory, every knockout of a white boxer and every new sprint record and every long run from scrimmage, Negroes saw a tiny step forward for Negroes in their everyday relations with the white majority. As Stuckey says, "They tended to regard individual achievements as progress for the race as a whole." What they did not realize was that the white American was able to compartmentalize his attitude about the Negro, to admire his exploits on the field but put him in the back of the bus on the way home. The white American expected the Negro to perform, to put out, but after he had showered and shaved, he was supposed to know his place. The white sports establishment would tell him where to go, what to do and how to do it. If he expressed any ideas of his own, any individual attitudes, he was promptly set down.

The case of Jesse Owens, who is now regarded as an Uncle Tom by militant Negroes, is illustrative. Less than a day after winning his fourth gold medal in the Olympic stadium in Berlin in 1936, Owens was sent on a European exhibition tour by the Amateur Athletic Union. He brought himself to the edge of exhaustion by running eight times in 10 days. Ordered to Sweden to race again for the greater financial glory of the AAU, he refused. Not long after, he was thrown out of amateur sports for life, and he rattled around places like Mexico City and Albuquerque, running against motorcycles, horses, anything but humans. This was his penalty for "irresponsibility."

"The black athlete was always expected by the honkie to play the role of the responsible Negro, the good Negro, no matter what else was going on in the black world," says Harry Edwards. "If blacks were being shot down in the street, the black athlete was expected to go ahead and play his basketball game and be quiet.

You know, the team spirit above all else. What about human rights? Forget about it. The black athlete was the institutionalized Tom, the institutionalized traitor, the white man's nigger."

This old-style black athlete may still be seen, in pre-packaged form, in the Harlem Globetrotters, the white man's favorite black road show. The Trotters help to perpetuate the Negro stereotype. Running about the court emitting savage jungle yells, shouting in thick Southern accents ("Yassuh, yassuh!"), pulling sly larcenous tricks like walking with the ball when the (white) referee's back is turned, calling one another inane names like Sweetwater and Showboat, they come across as frivolous, mildly dishonest children, the white man's encapsulated view of the whole Negro race set to the bouncy rhythms of their theme song, *Sweet Georgia Brown*. Says Willie Worsley, a member of the University of Texas at El Paso (then Texas Western) national championship basketball team of 1966, "The Trotters are clowns, and some of the young Negroes don't like it. We figure the Trotters are acting like clowns because they're black. They're acting like white people think black people should act. If you turned the Harlem Globetrotters white overnight, they wouldn't draw the manager the next night. But since they're out there doing what the white people like to think Negroes do, they're popular. Clowning like animals. Acting the fool. Cheating and screaming. They're out there telling the whites exactly what the whites want to hear."

Willie Worsley talks this way and sees these things because he is representative of the new Negro athlete. If he is sometimes truculent and suspicious, he is always dignified and proud. He has the "Negro instant" attitude.

Warren McVea, an alumnus of the University of Houston, defines Negro instant. "It means that in anything involving my people, I don't think twice. It's 'Negro instant.' As long as I have that attitude, I won't run into any problems with my own people."

The first requirement of this new Negro athlete with his new attitude is a pride in things black, in black ways of acting and thinking—not the old darky stereotypes with their laziness and duplicity and connivery, but the grace that the black man brings to sports.

"Take those great football teams of Michigan State," says Sam Skinner, Negro sports editor of San Francisco's *Sun-Reporter*. "Bubba Smith and his boys used to bring their record players and play soul music. Now this is better than a pep talk. Listening to James Brown is better than listening to Duffy Daugherty."

Says Harry Edwards: "Black people are communal by culture. They prepare communally. They dance, they play games communally. That slap on the hand you saw Lew Alcindor give Mike Warren or vice versa, that means something to those brothers. It means something to the brothers in the stands. It means something to the brothers who were watching the TV sets. The white cracker who walks over and slaps somebody's hand, that doesn't mean anything to him. He is mimicking something he doesn't even understand or feel."

Ronald Fair, the Negro novelist, believes that the black athlete, with his superior skills and proud new attitude, is still a dominant figure in the Negro struggle for equality—but with a difference. "Jim Brown can move as many people as James Baldwin," Fair says. "He probably moves *more* people than Baldwin." But the approach is new. Fair made the hero of his novel *Hog Butcher* an 18-

year-old athlete, but in this book the black hero is bold; he speaks out. "It's sad," Fair says, "but the Negro athlete used to be afraid to do this. He was afraid he'd lose his position. He's not afraid anymore."

Knowing how much potential influence he has in the Negro community, the new black athlete rejects the old thesis that every victory for the black competitor represents a step forward for the great mass of Negroes. "They are unwilling to equate personal success with racial success," says Sterling Stuckey, who has taught history at the University of Illinois at Chicago Circle. "The young black intellectual knows that individual success—for himself or for Negro athletes—means very little to the progress of the race. Those who hold the old view are continuing the oppression of the black race. They're being bought off."

Nowadays, as the thinking black athlete well knows, the Negro community will respect the black competitor only if the athlete does not confine his activities to the field. "There is a growing demand that the athlete take part in the affairs of the Negro community, that he use his prestige, the position he's acquired, to make himself a force in the improvement of the position of all Negroes," says Bob Wheeler, assistant superintendent of Kansas City public schools. "Negroes are apt to show hostility to a Negro athlete who doesn't take full advantage of his opportunities."

"The black athlete has finally realized he's got to have some kind of life when he takes that uniform off," says Bernie Casey of the Los Angeles Rams. "For many years, he suffered from delusions. He said, 'I'll just play the game and get my money and be a good nigger.' But the Negro is aware now that the house nigger is dead. Anyone who chooses to be one will find his fate is death. I'm not speaking of physical death, but of spiritual death, which could be the worst of all."

Militants like Harry Edwards reserve their harshest criticism for blacks who refuse to speak out, who remain "house niggers." Edwards professes to prefer Governor George Wallace of Alabama. "At least we know where Wallace stands, and at least he's not afraid to say what he thinks," Edwards told an audience. His voice drips with sarcasm and derision when he talks about certain mild-mannered Negro athletes. "As long as you have black athletes making it to the top and then shutting up like Willie Mays, or like Jesse Owens or Joe Louis, well, then athletics has done very little for the black community. It has helped black individuals to delude themselves, this is all. But when you have people speaking out like Jackie Robinson, Bill Russell and Oscar Robertson, you begin to feel the importance of sports to the black community. When you have people like Satch Sanders of the Celtics going out and getting a million-dollar grant from the federal government to revitalize housing in the black community of Boston— well, they didn't give it to him because he was some Joe off the street, but because he was Satch Sanders and because he had made himself a public figure and had access to the white man's media and public-opinion forces. He didn't have to speak out. He could have stayed home and been a Tom like the others."

Another spokesman for this new sense of community is Curtis McClinton of the Kansas City Chiefs. School administrator Bob Wheeler talks about the Chiefs' running back: "Negroes take pride in his exploits on the field, but they admire him equally, if not more, because he's churning like mad to make himself felt in the affairs of the community. It's no longer just a matter of a Negro athlete going to speak at schools. A man like McClinton works from morning to night on Negro problems. He's always there, always available to do whatever is asked of him. He's organizing a bank, doing other things to improve the economic position of the Negro. The same sort of admiration is now being given to Jim Brown. It's a wholly different feeling from what Negroes felt for Joe Louis. They still admire Joe, but they admire him almost completely for his exploits in the ring."

Curtis McClinton may have the "Negro instant" attitude, but he is no wild-eyed rabble-rouser urging Negroes automatically and indiscriminately to fight the white man with guns and bombs. He is no Rap Brown, no Stokely Carmichael, and indeed he is no Harry Edwards. When a group of black students began a march on the city hall of riot-torn Kansas City after the assassination of Martin Luther King, McClinton gathered up two of his colleagues, Buck Buchanan and Otis Taylor, and met the angry youngsters on the steps. He told them he understood their frustrations and their anger, that he felt the same shock and sorrow about the murder of Dr. King. But he added: "Our move at this time has to be one of dignity and pride befitting a man that has carried the torch of pride and love to all mankind. If there ever occurs a situation that will not be one of love and peace, separate yourself from it!" Later he led a group of demonstrators and would-be rioters to a local television station, where he rolled up his sleeves and acted as moderator of a forum in which Negroes expressed their hopes and their grievances to a predominantly white audience for nearly two hours.

24

The example of men like Curtis McClinton and the exhortations of men like Harry Edwards are making it almost impossible for the Negro athlete to remain simply an athlete, reveling in his sports achievements and going home at night with a feeling that he has advanced his race. "There are pressures pulling the Negro athletes," says Joe Pollock, a front-office spokesman for the St. Louis Cardinals' football team, which suffered its own racial upheaval during the 1967 season. (Black players, smarting under a range of grievances from race-baiting on the part of white teammates to discrimination by coaches on the field, filed a written bill of particulars with the Cardinal management that stirred up a whirlwind of controversy when it leaked out to the St. Louis papers.) "It's damned tough to be a middle-of-the-road Negro these days. It's almost impossible. You've got to be one way or the other, and a lot of these guys don't really want to be one way or the other."

The Negro star who refuses to take a firm stand on racial matters finds himself at worst ostracized by his race, consigned to Bernie Casey's "spiritual death," or at best left in a kind of limbo between white and black. Some, like Willie Mays, still try to take refuge in a passive role. Willie gives money to Negro causes, but he is not the most likely candidate to be leading a black boycott on the San Francisco Giants. "I'm a ballplayer," Mays says. "I am not a politician or a writer or a historian. I can do best for my people by doing what I do best. If I can provide pleasure for those who like my game, then I believe I am bringing pride to those of my race, as well as myself."

More and more, Willie Mays finds himself becoming what Mike Garrett of the Chiefs calls "a marginal man," exciting the deep respect of neither race, and indeed, the outright dislike of some members of both. For a long time, Garrett, the Heisman Trophy winner from the University of Southern California, was falling into the same limbo. "I didn't fit into the slum that I came from, and I didn't fit into the white-oriented social world of USC with its emphasis on fraternity row," Garrett recalls. "I was a marginal man. And when I became a professional football player I felt the same way, only more so. As a football star I felt cut off from the Negro world I came from. The Negroes of Boyle Heights in Los Angeles would say to me, 'You have left us,' and the white world says to me, 'We don't want you yet in our world.' "

Like many other black athletes, Garrett is stepping out of his limbo and taking firm stands on black-and-white matters. He does not hesitate to speak up when he sees what he regards as racial inequities on or off the playing field. And he has made a personal commitment. "As a Negro celebrity," he says, "I know that I must go back and help less fortunate Negroes, even though in my heart I may not want to." Mike Garrett's "marginal" days are coming to an end. He is responding to pressures on the Negro athlete. He is becoming the proud new black who is reworking the future of his race, rendering the "house nigger" all but obsolete, and turning the world of sports upside down in the process.

"He Can Get Ahead
if He Tries": The Unknown
Price of Success

2

What is happening today amounts to a revolt by the black athlete against the framework and attitudes of American sport. To the white sports follower this upheaval has come as a surprise; the man in the grandstand, comfortable in his feeling that sports is his own pet province, accustomed to regarding the Negro athlete as a symbol of integration, has failed to see the disillusion beneath the surface. He knows nothing about the blacks whom he professes to understand, for a wall of misapprehension and apathy cuts the white off from the realities of the black athlete's background and hopes.

Two of the most celebrated college basketball players of 1967-1968 serve as examples. One is Don Smith, Iowa State All-America, ghetto-born and bred to trouble. He was the pride of a campus that would have been stunned if it had ever heard him tell the story of his youth. The other is Elvin Hayes of the University of Houston, the famed "Big E," a small-town Southern Negro, the product of an astonishing family headed by a woman of enormous dedication, and a man searching his own route through the black-white maze.

What does the white man cheering in the grandstand know of Don Smith or Elvin Hayes? Not a thing—and that is part of the shame. Now meet them.

Don Smith fidgeted nervously on the bench. Iowa State had just lost to Kansas State in the crucial game of the season, and ever since the final horn had blown in the big armory in Ames, Iowa, the students and fans had been sitting patiently in their seats. This had been the last home game for Smith, a light-skinned Negro from the slums of Brooklyn, and statisticians were already busy working out the summation of his brilliant college athletic career. It had developed that he was the second best Big Eight rebounder of all time, behind Bill Bridges, and the third best Big Eight scorer, behind Clyde Lovellette and Bob Boozer. He had been All-Conference each year, Sophomore of the Year in 1966 and Big Eight Player of the Year in 1968. He had made the Helms Foundation first-string All-America and half a dozen other All-Americas as well. Earlier in the season he had matched up against the formidable Lew Alcindor of UCLA, scoring 33 points and picking up 12 rebounds. Somebody once asked Alcindor what he thought of Elvin Hayes of Houston. "He's one of the best," said the taciturn Lew, "along with Don Smith of Iowa State."

Now Smith waited shyly in the armory while his jersey was officially retired. The admiring student body presented him with a plaque, the mayor of Ames gave him a handsome piece of luggage, and Dr. W. Robert Parks, the university president, handed the young athlete a color photograph of himself in action. Smith said only a few words in response. He said he was grateful for the gifts and for his years at Iowa State. Mostly, he said, he was sorry he had missed three free throws in the last six minutes.

"Just like him," said an instructor in the audience. "Everybody's telling him how great he is and he's apologizing for missing free throws."

28

Another spectator, sitting alongside the instructor, agreed. "Yeah, for a shine, that is one good boy."

As Don Smith tells it: "The first house we lived in in Brooklyn was a second-floor apartment at 454 Vanderbilt. It belonged to my grandmother. My mother and father were separated, and I slept alone in the living room, and nine others slept in the two bedrooms. It was a typical ghetto house with roaches and rats and mice and everything else you can imagine. When I was little, it was hard to get into the house, because of what was going on downstairs. There was a restaurant downstairs that used to have a jukebox playing, and dope addicts and drunks—in the halls. People used to get shot and stabbed right on my street; and there were prostitutes all around, but this didn't bother me—they were just making a living. I remember the roaches better than the prostitutes. I guess I ate quite a few roaches; our cabinets were infested. One day I was gonna have a bowl of cereal, and I put my hand into a box and a mouse bit my finger. I also remember this dog we had, named Lady, and no one used to take her out, so she used to 'do it' on the floor, and I couldn't stand that.

"When I was eleven, we moved to a project at 135 Richards Street in the Red Hook section of Brooklyn. I went with my mother and my sister and brother. This was a better apartment than the other one, but we only stayed a year, because I got us kicked out. If you get an accumulation of fines, they kick you out. You used to get fines for messing with the elevators, or being on the grass or on the roof. We were kids, and we played football on the grass, and that was illegal. We were supposed to play at the park, but that was usually taken by the older people. We used to go on the roof to look around, and we used to stop the elevators between floors and drink wine. One day I was gone to this rock 'n' roll show in Manhattan, and when I came home that night and knocked on the door there was no answer. So I went outside and climbed up this lamppost and looked inside and saw that there was no furniture, so I took it for granted we had been kicked out. I went to my grandmother's house, and sure enough—everybody was there.

"They started calling me 'Duck' because my feet were

so big. One of my friends was Cemetery and another was Knife, because he always looked so sharp, and another was Nutt. Cemetery is now a Muslim. I don't know where Knife is. Nutt died of an overdose about three years ago, and some of the guys are still on the corner, drinking wine and taking dope.

"The first junior high school I went to was P.S. 9, but I got kicked out because I was implicated in a stealing incident. A friend of mine saw this pocketbook and told me to get between him and the teacher. I was blocking and he took the money. About an hour later some detectives came to school and wanted to know who took the money, so they put everybody in the auditorium and searched us. For some reason they picked me and the other guy out and we told them we had stolen it and we were sorry. We got kicked out of school.

"I didn't have any thoughts at all about stealing. It was like a game to me, played by just about everybody. I remember the first thing I stole was twenty dollars from my grandmother, and that was when I was eight. The first thing I remember stealing from the outside was a Slinky—one of those toys that goes down stairs. It was a big deal. I had a lot of fun with it.

"As a kid I was always out. When I would go to Manhattan it usually was to steal. I used to take anything I could get my hands on: jewelry and toys. I used to keep them or sell them. I used to keep the baseballs I stole, and play with them. If I couldn't steal anything else, I'd steal Hershey bars—just to be stealing something. When I would get caught in a store, I wouldn't go back; I would go steal somewhere else. They wouldn't press any charges; they would just tell me not to do it again. I used to stay out all night and sell newspapers on the subway. I stole the papers off the back of a truck and sold them for five cents or six cents each to the passengers on the A train.

"I hardly even knew there was a white community or a white society. When we watched TV it was another world and it never dawned on me that this was reality. Once when I was about ten I was hitching a ride on the back of a bus and a white cop saw me and told me to get off and stop. I got off and ran and he ran after me. He hit me on the neck with his billy club and yelled, 'Stop, you black nigger!' This was really the first time that I knew there were two worlds. Later, when I was around fourteen, we were stealing in a bakery, and a cop came up and told us to stop. We ran and he shot up in the air and we stopped. I was arrested a lot of times. Once I was arrested for jimmying open a parking meter. They sent me to the Youth House for about two months. It was nice. They had food. They had three meals a day. They taught lessons, and you had your own room.

"When I was sixteen I used to hang out with this guy who burglarized houses. One day someone saw him up on the fire escape in a Jewish neighborhood. A friend and I were sitting down waiting for him to come down, and the cops picked us all up. They asked us if we knew anything, and we denied it. Then they took us down to the police station and beat us with their fists. *Huge* cops. When we would say we knew nothing they would hit us in the face with these big fists. So we told. I went to jail for two months after that. I didn't like it at all. Hardened criminals were there. The police used to say that I was so bad I was going to wind up in the chair.

"I smoked pot in high school, but I think I did it just because everybody was doing it. I used to get a five-dollar bag that would make twenty joints. I never did get into the heroin stage. A lot of my friends are now junkies out on the street. We used to fight a white gang called the Hilltoppers all the time. I used a car aerial or a Molotov cocktail. We had zip guns and twenty-two's. Once in a while somebody would get killed. One day I dropped my guard and went out in the wrong territory, and another gang, the Chaplains, caught me and stomped me.

"The last time I stole was in high school. Some friends and I mugged a white man looking for a black prostitute. We got three-hundred and twenty dollars. I was an average kid on the block. The bad kids would mug people all the time. I just did it on weekends."

This was the Don Smith, grown into a 6-foot-7-inch, 193-pound All-City center who won a scholarship to play basketball at Iowa State. At the end of the last col-   31 lege game he played, Smith's chilling boyhood was not on the minds of the fans in the field house listening to the tributes being paid to him. This ghetto child had done his best for Iowa State: All-America, Big Eight Player of the Year. But had being a star on the court transformed him into an accepted, respected human being? Far from it.

Life in Smith's freshman dormitory was typical of all his four college years. He moved in with a white roommate who had a farming background. "Every weekend he'd go home," Smith recalls, "and he'd leave little notes behind, like 'Don't touch my razor!' It was always don't touch this or don't touch that. One day I saw something he'd written, and it said how hard it was for him to live with a nigger."

And so later that evening of his last home game, after hearing himself lauded and appreciated—an evening that would have set up a white athlete for life— Smith was not particularly excited. He reckoned that of all the white people he had met in that strange flatland of Iowa, only two had been sincere. He still felt awkward around whites. He still did not trust them. He felt good about his education (which he planned to complete for his degree), and his exceptional basketball ability had earned him a contract with the Cincinnati Royals. But he would not recommend Iowa State as a place for a black athlete—at least for a black athlete who wanted to be happy.

Elvin Hayes is, as they like to say down in Houston, something else. One night when the University of Houston basketball team was flying home from another successful appearance on the road, a newspaperman aboard the plane tried to get Elvin's attention. "Hey, boy!" the reporter called.

A silence came over the cabin. Players stopped what they were doing, refreshments were poised in mid-air, and conversations ceased. The "Big E" turned to the reporter and said softly: "Boy's on *Tarzan*. *Boy* plays on *Tarzan*. I'm no boy. I'm twenty-two years old. I worked hard to become a man. I don't call you boy."

"I'm sorry," the newspaperman said. "I didn't mean anything by it."

"I hope not," Hayes said, and the plane relaxed.

Elvin Hayes does not take part in boycotts; he does not make loud demands on the white athletic establishment; he does not proselytize younger Negro athletes to take up arms against the inequities that visit the Negro in sports. He sympathizes and understands and respects the militant Negro athletes, but he has chosen a different path for himself.

Elvin Hayes is eight inches over six feet tall, 240 pounds in weight, dark coffee in color. He is broad and thick in the nose and lips, and his eyes are set so wide apart that you often feel that you are only talking to half of him. He wears a small mustache and his hair is cropped close to his skull. He has a bright, flashing smile, but he does not throw it around indiscriminately. The smile of Elvin Hayes does not appear the instant a white man says hello. It must be earned. There is about him a massive dignity that comes only partly from his height. In a roomful of Negroes and whites he stands apart, a figure of total independence. "You couldn't imagine him stepping into the gutter and letting some bully pass, even in the old days," Wells Twombly wrote in the *Houston Chronicle*.

For three years Elvin Hayes was the hero of Houston, admired and respected by black and white alike. He was always the last Cougar to be introduced over the P.A. system before each home game, and by the time the second or third man had been introduced, the chant of "E . . . E . . . E" had become so loud that the other players' names were lost. When Elvin would finally detach his long body from the bench, throw down the polka-dot towel that was a team trademark and amble out on the floor in his size 16s, the cheering made the needles on the volume-indicator meters in the radio booth jump across the red line.

Then Elvin used up his last semester of eligibility. He ignored the local professional basketball team, the Houston Mavericks of the ABA and signed for an estimated $440,000 with the NBA's San Diego Rockets. The folks who used to chant "E . . . E . . . E" took a new view of him. Letters to the editors began mentioning how ungrateful Elvin had become. Fans would call radio programs and air their objections to the way their former hero had ignored the offers of the Houston Mavericks. The street corner conversations were more to the point. "I used to think he knew his place," a cab driver said, "but now he's acting like one of your smart-ass Northern jigs." A Houston reporter summed up the attitude of the townsfolk: "When Elvin was representing the University of Houston on the court, he was called 'a credit to his race.' But when he signed with the San Diego team, he became another 'smart nigger.' Houston's attitude about him turned just like that." And once again that familiar cry was heard in the land: "Sports has been good to him. He should be more grateful to the people who made him." One is reminded of a re-

34

mark made long ago by the heavyweight champion of the rational world. "Who made me is *me*," said Cassius Clay with authority. Who made Elvin Hayes of Rayville, Louisiana, is Elvin Hayes.

Rayville is a town in northeast Louisiana about 60 miles upcountry from Waterproof, four miles from Bee Bayou, just down the road from Alto and Holly Ridge. Its 5,000 residents, divided about 50-50 racially, work in small businesses, cotton gins, a clothing mill or two. The farms around Rayville are tilled by machines nowadays; hundreds of former field hands, Negroes almost to the last man, have gone away to places like Dallas and Los Angeles and Chicago seeking work. In 1969 one of the local schools will drop agriculture as a course; "Ag" used to be the mainstay of the curriculum. Signs on the post-office bulletin board advise young residents that the U.S. Army is "a wise choice," and others say, "Go Air Force." These are two labor markets that are still hiring. Now that cotton has ended a way of life, the Negro youth of Rayville have a tendency to rattle around in meaningless pursuits.

Racially, Rayville is relaxed, as Southern towns go. The big midtown high school has been integrated for several years, although hardly any Negroes elect to attend. The malt and sundae stand on the corner of Madeline and Louisa Streets has one takeout window for whites and a separate one for Negroes, but no one gets upset about it. "You have to expect that in a Southern town," says Elvin Hayes's sister, Bunnatine. "It doesn't bother us. We go elsewhere. You have to make up your mind about things like that." For the most part, the two races mind their own business in Rayville.

Now that Elvin Hayes is a famous All-America basketball player, everyone in Rayville professes to be his dear friend, his old acquaintance. "Ah've known Elving all his laff," says a white man at the Rayville Motel, at the west end of town. "Fan boy, fan family." Later, someone passes the remark along to James P. Smith, principal of the all-black Eula D. Britton school, where Elvin attended class. James Smith explodes in a big laugh and says, "That white man doesn't know Elvin or anybody else on this side of town. This is a different world."

The "different world" is the east part of Rayville, literally the other side of the tracks, where black families live in homes ranging from shacks to a few fairly comfortable family dwellings. The Hayes family is better off than most. You walk across a few wooden boards that span a gully and you are on the front steps of the rectangular frame house at 603 Texas Street. There are no sidewalks. The Hayes house is not fancy; the ceiling sags, and now and then a leak has to be patched, but there is space and order and warmth and a matriarch who runs the show. Mrs. Savannah Hayes, mother of Elvin and five others, sits in a stiff-backed chair in the living room and explains how and why she and her late husband sent their six children to college: "I been in the fields. Raised on a farm. My daddy worked another man's land. I chopped cotton and I picked cotton. Before I was married I always said, 'if I ever own a family, I want them to have a better chance than I have.' Well, I married a man who felt the same way. Chris Hayes. A powerful man. He had a fourth-grade education, but he'd traveled all around the world as a fireman on a ship, and he'd learned a few things. We settled here, and he began firing the boilers at the Union [cotton] Compress, and when the children came along, he'd tell 'em: 'I'll wear overalls for you if you'll go to school, but if *you* won't, I won't!' And what he wasn't telling them, I was. I'd say, 'Look, if you go to school I'll be with you all the way, but if you don't go to school, you'll have to go out on your own—because I'm not going to take care of you so you can run in the streets.' So we started sending our children off to college one by one, and my husband worked two jobs to pay for it. Sometimes three jobs. Some days I'd put on overalls and fire them boilers myself—I can do it as good as anybody else, and I have did it many times! Even after my husband had a heart attack, you couldn't stop him. And when he lay on his death bed, he said to me, 'Don't feel like everything gonna be done when I'm gone. Keep them children in school! The Lawd's gonna make a way for you to do it.' Well, the Lawd did. Four of our children were either in or through college, and that left Bunnatine and Elvin. Bunnatine got a full academic scholarship to Southern University and Elvin got a full athletic scholarship to Houston, and that made it six out of six."

"My father used to try to pass his knowledge along to us," recalls Elvin's oldest sister, Christine Hayes Minor, who holds a master's degree from the University of Wisconsin. "I remember him telling me, 'You can kill a man, but you can't take the knowledge away from him. I admire the Jews. Even though people have prejudice against the Jews, they have to recognize their knowledge. Until the Negro achieves knowledge, then he will not be able to attain recognition. It's not that the Jews are any more intelligent, but they read and

37

they study.' And then he'd send me off to read. By the
time I finished the eighth grade, I had read all of Shake-
speare's plays. I didn't understand them too well, but
I'd read them."

Elvin was the baby of the family, and by the time he
entered the Eula D. Britton school a few blocks from
his home, the Hayes pattern of academic excellence
had been firmly established. For a while, the tradition
worked against the gangly boy. At seven, he had told
an aunt that his ambition was to be "a noble man."

"You're not gonna be anything," the aunt chided the
boy. "Look at you, all arms and elbows."

"Yes, I am," Elvin insisted. "Someday I'm gonna be
a noble man."

But in school he was deeply troubled by the idea
that too much was expected of him, that he would be
judged by the records of his five older brothers and sisters and found wanting. "And my mother used to be on
me all the time," Elvin says. "She'd say, 'If you don't
do well, you're not gonna stay around my house!' She'd
say, 'You're the last one and you're not gonna be a failure!' Like, a lot of times I didn't want to go to school
and I used to come back home and my mother'd send
me straight back down there. I used to think she was
real hard on me. I'd say, 'I'm not Bunny! I can't do
what the others did,' and she'd say 'Yes, you can!' and I
would have to go back and try."

Elvin's marks remained poor though passing, and his
personality problem became more severe. "My sister
Bunnatine came just before me, and she was valedicto-
rian, and all my brothers and sisters had made straight
A averages, and I just said to myself, 'Well, I'm not
gonna do it.' It wasn't that I didn't have the ability,

but I was trying to do things in my own way. Everybody was surprised when they gave an I.Q. test and I had the highest in my class. But I didn't want people saying, 'Ah, he thinks he's smart.' I tried to keep people from noticing me. Then they couldn't look at me and say, 'Oh, here's another member of the Hayes family. What's he gonna do? Oh, he probably won't do nothing!' "

Mrs. Savannah Hayes well remembers the device Elvin put up to help him retreat from the troubling reality around him. "Oh, how I *do* remember!" Mrs. Hayes says. "He put up a bucket with a hole in the bottom, right on a beautiful water elm I had in the back of the house, and he threw a rubber ball into that bucket and stomped around that tree and dried the ground out till he killed it. Killed my beautiful water elm! Then he hung the bucket on the side of the house and kept right on throwing the ball into it."

"Well, a kid in my neighborhood had to play outside or not at all," Elvin recalls. "We didn't have the facilities that other kids have. No concrete to play on. No baskets to shoot at. I cut the bottom out of this old bucket. My basketball was one of those five-and-ten-cent-store rubber balls about the size of a softball. I lallygagged around with balls like that right through high school. People say, 'Wouldn't that ruin your game, throwing the wrong kind of ball at the wrong kind of basket?' But no, it didn't. If you could dribble that little ball across that uneven dirt, you'd never have trouble on a basketball court."

Elvin's idol and model was Bill Russell. All day long he would stand under the bucket, perfecting moves designed to confound the great Boston Celtic center. "Once in a while I'd see him bouncing that ball," says his high-school coach, Melvin Rogers, "and he'd spin to his left and shoot a basket, and he'd say to me, 'Bill Russell got me to the right, so I hooked to the left!' That's all he had on his mind: Bill Russell. If there was a President of the United States, Elvin didn't know it."

In the eighth grade, Elvin was still playing the role of the child who wanted to be different from his brothers and sisters, and he had started running with a bad crowd. "I became tough, and they had to put me in a special section of my class. But while I was running with that crowd I learned a lot about kids that they called bad. Nobody understood those kids. Nobody took the time. A lot of them had no other way to be noticed. They were poor; they had no books in their house; they had bad backgrounds. The only way they could be noticed in the world and get any attention at all was to be bad, to do mischievous things. They had no interest in school, because school offered them nothing. Like, maybe some of them would have liked to study automobile body work, but there were no automobile bodies in school to work on."

Elvin had not been in with the "bad" crowd for long when he came under the influence of the Reverend Dr. John Calvin, a former dean of men at Grambling College in Grambling, Louisiana. "Dr. Calvin showed me that someone understood me, and he made me realize that someone was willing to give me their hand and help me. He told me it was fine for me to want to be a basketball player but I couldn't if I didn't study. He told me that the two things went together. This was the eighth grade. This was the turning point. From then on I started bearing down. From then on it was nothing but study and practice, study and practice."

At first, Elvin was too gawky and clumsy to count for much in the free ebb and flow of a basketball game. "They used him on a neighborhood team just so they'd have the full five men," his sister Christine says, chortling at the memory. "He'd fall all over himself when the ball came to him. We were so embarrassed! Every time they threw the ball to Elvin, he'd miss it." He was cut from the freshman team and he spent that whole summer shooting baskets. He shot 11 hours a day. Eleven. He is sure, because it is not the kind of thing you forget. "That boy worked," says Melvin Rogers.

"When I finally made the high-school team," Elvin recalls, "the fans would holler, 'Take him out! Take him out!' I was growing fast and I had coordination problems. And I didn't have the money for the right equipment. One time I started a game with two right shoes—my own had fallen apart and these were all I could find lying around."

"He finally pulled himself together in the eleventh grade," says Melvin Rogers, known to everyone in black Rayville as "Cawch." "Understand, he was no ball of fire. He was like any big tall boy who doesn't know his hands from his feet. He used to stumble over the center line! And Bill Russell was always in his mind. His thinking skipped college. In his thinking he saw himself playing against Russell right away. College was just a means to that. That's why I knew this year that there wasn't a chance that Elvin would sign with the Houston Mavericks. There's no Bill Russell in that league!"

Louisiana maintains the segregation of the races by having white high-school teams play in one grouping and black in another, and Eula D. Britton High School won the black championship behind its superstar Elvin

Hayes in his senior year. The University of Houston offered him a full athletic scholarship, and Elvin went into a world that flabbergasted him. "I walked around the Houston campus without saying a word, because I had a speech problem. My speech problem was that I talked like a small-town Southern Negro. I mumbled my words and strung them together, and certain words like 'individual' and 'computer' I couldn't say at all. I still have trouble with those words. I spoke the way the kids of Rayville spoke, not the way English was spoken in my home. I mean, my sister the English teacher, she would speak perfect English around the house, but then I would go out and listen to the other kids on the street and that sounded good to me, jiving around with them. And then I couldn't get rid of it in college. So I decided to major in speech education, for two reasons. One was to help myself. The other was to try to help other kids with the same problem."

On the campus at Houston, Elvin Hayes seemed to carry his stern mother perched on his shoulder. Ted Nance, the university's sports publicist, remembers when someone offered Elvin a cigarette, and Elvin backed away as though in deep shock and said, "My mother'd whip me if she saw me with a cigarette!"

He attended classes and studied his lessons as though his only chance to go up against Bill Russell lay in getting straight A's in every subject. His diligence astounded his professors. One of them said to athletic director Harry Fouke: "That big tall boy showed up this morning looking a little groggy. I checked and found that the freshman team played last night at Henderson. The game was over at ten and the bus got back to Houston around two-thirty in the morning and there

42

he was, right on time for my eight o'clock class!"

At first Elvin could not accustom himself to the attitude of the big city crowds. In Louisiana he had played before mostly Negro audiences, and they had viewed him as both athlete and human being. But in Houston the crowd seemed to expect him to be all athlete, to approach perfection. Elvin and Don "Duck" Chaney of Baton Rouge, Louisiana, were the first Negroes ever to play basketball for a University of Houston team, and they were cheered and praised and patted when the game went well. "But if we had a little off night, the crowds would get on us more than the other players," Elvin says. "Duck and I could be hurt or sick or just off our game and the people would cut loose on us. They expected us to be terrific every minute."

Off the court, Elvin's size and his personal dignity held racial incidents to a minimum, though one of his teammates forgot himself one night after a game and muttered the word "nigger."

"We sat right down and talked about it," Elvin says. "He explained that it was just something he had in his vocabulary and it slipped out. It's not something you can break overnight. So we discussed why he said it, where it came from, what it meant to the whites and what it meant to the Negroes. That talk went on for a long time, and I think it changed that guy's mind. I think he became a different person."

Four years at the University of Houston crystallized Elvin Hayes's own thinking about race, caste, delinquency and the problems of poverty. He married Erna Livingston as a junior and became a father as a senior ("We call ourselves the triple E: me, Erna and little Elvin"), and except for his appearances in class and on the court, he seldom was seen about the campus. "People would ask me where I was keeping myself, and I'd just shrug and say, 'Around.'"

Elvin was keeping himself in Houston's black ghetto, jiving around with the poor boys of grammar- and high-school age. "It's like this," he says. "Before I got into basketball in high school, nobody noticed me, nobody cared anything about me. Then you play on a team, and they get to know you, and then everybody wants to be with you. And then they start saying to you, 'Why are you running with those bad guys, those bums from the poor neighborhood? You should look over those guys!' But that's why they're bad guys! Because everybody looked over them! The only way they can be seen is by fights or troublemaking, and then people say, 'Oh, he's bad!' So I go down there and try to correspond to those kids, to show them that somebody cares for them like Reverend Calvin cared for me, to show them that they have a place in life just like everybody else.

"But when I first started doing this in Houston, the better-off people would ask me what I was doing hanging around the poor. They'd say, 'Why do you do that? Those people are below your class.' Well, I feel that you have no class. Now I can go anywhere I want, but I prefer the poor people. You should see the change that comes over these kids when they find out you care. They come up to me and they say, 'I can't believe you'd talk to me. Why do you talk to me?' And I say, 'I talk to you because I'm no different than you are.' And that's what people can do nowadays. That's what whites can do too. Just go around caring about people and instilling some truth into the younger heads. Tell them from birth why discrimination is wrong, how the world

44

can be better. Put out their hands. Trouble is, nowadays when some of the Negroes put out their hands, they get 'em slapped, and then they're ready to resort to violence. A man gets tired of being pushed around. But the violence isn't for me. It's not my way. All I'm trying to do is be a good man myself and just wait and see what happens."

Not long ago Melvin Rogers was sitting at his over-crowded desk in the Eula D. Britton High School, when the telephone rang. "It was Elvin calling long distance," says Coach Rogers. "He had just signed a contract with the San Diego team, and he wanted to know what the kids needed back home. I asked him, 'Elvin, what helped you the most in school?' He said, 'The recreation program. What does it need?' I said, 'Well, we have an old building here that could be turned into a recreation hall with card tables and pool tables and Ping-Pong tables, so kids wouldn't have to go downtown to the pool hall. And we need a hard-surface court with basketball nets all around.'

"And you know what Elvin said? Well, if you do know him, I don't have to tell you. He said, 'Wait right there, Cawch, wait right there! You'll have baskets all over the place!'" Elvin Hayes wants to save the remaining water elms in the quiet town of his childhood.

In his determination to work among the Negro poor, to unlock the tongues of mumbly-jumbly black children in the South, Elvin Hayes is perfectly typical of the new Negro athlete, whose commitments extend far beyond a lime-washed goal line or an outfield fence 356 feet away. But in other respects, the Elvin Hayes story can be misleading. It can be employed, in fact, to buttress certain theories that have been used to keep   **45** the Negro in bondage since the Emancipation Procla-mation. A white traveling salesman in Tupelo, Mis-sissippi, makes the case on behalf of millions of racists: "Look at that Elvin Hayes. Started with nothing. Family had nothing. Came from the deep South, where we're supposed to be mistreating the Nigras. And look what happens? He gets a college education and then gets a four-hundred-and-forty-thousand-dollar deal. It just goes to show you: a Nigra *can* get ahead if he tries. Trouble is, most of them would rather sit around collecting wel-fare checks."

It is perfectly true that the Negro "can get ahead if he tries"—if the Negro is a highly gifted athlete like Elvin Hayes, if he has an iron-willed mother like Sa-vannah Hayes and a hard-working father like the late Chris Hayes, if he sprouts to 80 inches in height and has a fanatical determination to shoot baskets, if he has a patient coach like Melvin Rogers and an inspira-tion like the Reverend Dr. John Calvin, if he gets enough to eat, if he is not weakened by pellagra or worms, if he does not fall from rheumatic fever or pneumonia or any of the other diseases that seem to concentrate on Negro children, and a dozen or so other ifs. If the chain of ifs is not broken at any point, an Elvin Hayes may be produced. The yawning gulf that separates whites from blacks may be crossed.

3

The exploitation complained of by black athletes is an ugly word that suggests Negro sharecropping or school segregation. Few whites realize that on the campus it is often bound up with a kind of prejudice that is several degrees removed from whites-only swimming pools or overt job discrimination. This subtler prejudice grows out of a state of mind that does not even recognize itself as prejudice.

Rebellion, in its turn, is an emotion-charged word that suggests a response to a deliberate provocation (e.g., the overseer's whip). But in the spring of 1968 black athletes at the University of Texas at El Paso proved that this need not be so. Reacting at last to treatment by coaches and administration, Negroes flatly refused to participate in a scheduled college meet; they felt they were being exploited—consciously or unconsciously—and they rebelled. The setting was unusual.

El Paso lies farther west than Denver, Cheyenne or Dodge City. Although it is in Texas, it is nearly 1,000 miles away from the "grits zone"—that portion of the United States where hominy grits come with your breakfast whether you ordered them or not. El Paso is just about as far as you can go in Texas and not be in Mexico, old or New. Geographically, at least, the city should be relatively free of prejudice against Negroes, and for the most part it is. Negroes make up only about 2 per cent of the city's permanent population; the economic competition that aggravates the relationship of black to white is missing. And besides, there are the Mexican-Americans—some 45 per cent of the population—to siphon off racial prejudice.

The only conspicuous exception to El Paso's orderly Negro-and-white relations lies in parched foothills just to the north of the central business district. There, framed on the west by a horizon line of rocky desert, one finds an institution that calls itself by the long name of the University of Texas at El Paso; until 1967 it was known in sports circles, if not in academic, as Texas Western. Most people now call it UT-El Paso or simply UTEP, and its players are "The Miners."

You may be excused for assuming that UTEP is an all-Negro school. Many do. In fact, there is a story among UTEP athletes that a high-school football player recently turned down a UTEP recruiter, explaining that he did not count himself a bigot, but neither did he want to be the only white in an all-black school. He was surprised when the recruiter explained hastily that UTEP is almost entirely white, that there are fewer than 250 Negroes in the student body of almost 10,000.

The school's reputation for being all-black was firmly established in 1966, when its basketball team played the University of Kentucky in the nationally televised NCAA finals. Although UTEP (then still known as Texas Western) had white players on the bench, none played. The starting five were black, and the first two replacements were black, and they made a startling contrast to Adolph Rupp's lily-white aggregation from Lexington. They also beat the Kentuckians 72-65.

Of course, the idea of gaining a national reputation from the muscles and skills of Negro athletes was not new at UTEP in 1966. Long before that, the school had recruited Jim "Bad News" Barnes and many another excellent black athlete, starting with Charlie Brown in 1956. The walls around the university's athletic department are covered with pictures of Negroes who have brought glory to the school. In a glass trophy case at the place of honor in the hall is a huge oil painting by El Pasoan Tom Lea (author of *The Brave Bulls*) showing Negro end Bob Wallace catching the pass that defeated Utah in the last few seconds of a crucial game in the 1965 season. Farther down the hall is a two-by-three-foot photograph of Detroit Negro Bobby Joe Hill with basketball in hand, and other testimonials to the school's star black athletes: Orsten Artis, Dave Lattin, Fred Carr, Charlie West.

Under the leadership of an enterprising and popular president, named Dr. Joseph M. Ray, UTEP nearly doubled its enrollment in eight years, and even now the jackhammers are tearing up the campus, ripping out space for new buildings and additions to old ones. Dr. Ray, the athletic-minded professors at the school and the high-powered team of coaches admit that the exploits of the school's Negro athletes have not hampered the expansion program. "The Negro athlete has helped us tremendously," asserts coach Bobby Dobbs. "We wouldn't have built this institution as quickly without the Negro, because they have been very fine kids and we have been happy to have them." Dr. Ray himself says that UTEP would not be so well-known throughout the country without its black athletes, but he adds with pride, "It's not too wholesome to be known as a jockey strap college. We've got some quality undergirding this."

One might suppose that UTEP, with its famed Negro

basketball players, its Negro football stars and its predominantly Negro track team, would be trying to give its black athletes the squarest of square deals in appreciation for the achievements of the past and to assure a steady flow of black athletes in the future. One might suppose that the Negro athlete would be treated with a modicum of respect, if not reverence. But the Negroes on the campus insist they are not. For a starter, they wish that members of the UTEP athletic department would stop referring to them as "niggers."

"This was the first institution in Texas—right here!—that had a colored athlete, and George McCarty, our athletic director, was the coach who recruited him," says assistant athletic director Jim Bowden. "George McCarty's done more for the nigger race than Harry Edwards'll do if he lives to be a hundred."

In his pleasant office, short, bald-headed George McCarty sits under a wreath of his own cigar smoke and brags about the "nigger" athletes who have starred for the school. Occasionally he says "nigra." He seldom uses the word Negro, pronounced *knee-grow*, although sometimes he seems to try. "It's a habit that you don't change overnight," he explains.

Says Bob Wallace, the end who is featured in Tom Lea's oil painting, "When I go into the athletic office, McCarty says 'Negro,' but when you overhear him talking to somebody else it's always 'nigger' or 'nigra.' Jim Bowden's the same way, and so are some of the others. They can pronounce Negro if they want to. *They can pronounce it.* But I think it seems like such a little thing to them. The trouble with them is they're not thinking of the Negro and how he feels. Wouldn't you suppose that if there was one word these guys that live off Negroes would get rid of, one single word in the whole vocabulary, it would be *nigger?* But that's how much they think of us."

David "Big Daddy" Lattin of the Phoenix Suns, who played on the Miners' national championship team in 1966, says the problem is not a new one. "We had a meeting of the Negroes on the squad when I was a freshman, and that must have been 1963, and we decided to talk to McCarty about a few things. We said to him, 'Listen, man, either you get yourself together and learn how to pronounce that word or . . .!' "

McCarty remembers the incident. "They asked me about my enunciation of the word and I told them I do not do this intentionally. I told them that inopportunely I might say it that way but I didn't *mean* it that way, that it was no reflection on their race or their characters, and that I would try to change. But I couldn't seem to get out of the habit—I was born in the South, maybe that's what caused it. So they suggested that I say 'colored.' I tried that too. I told them I would try to watch myself, and I had been embarrassed a time or two before then, just in idle conversations. I've even said things in a joking manner when Charlie Brown was here —he was our first one—and I've even related a story that maybe was funny, but it wasn't funny to him, and then I'd have to turn around and apologize to him, because I didn't mean it that way at all."

For George McCarty the problem cannot seem a very significant one, and he certainly has no conception of how important it is to the players. McCarty waxes absolutely enthusiastic about the exploits of his Negro athletes and continually reminds the listener that Texas Western fielded the first integrated team in Texas. He is under the impression that the Negroes at UTEP think the world of him, and he can see why. To some he may be reminiscent of the apocryphal Southern senator who wrote a book about the greatness of the black race and titled it *Niggers I Have Known.*

Indeed, the establishment of the University of Texas at El Paso seems to reflect McCarty's attitude, or vice versa. Most of the school's administrators and teachers see themselves in the avant-garde in Negro-white relations. Dr. Ray has spoken of the national reputations the school has built for its black athletes, paving the way for their lucrative entry into professional sports. Dean of Students Jimmy Walker tells of the special consideration given to the problems of the Negroes on the campus. He is not insincere, nor is Dr. Ray, nor for that matter are McCarty or Jim Bowden. They may admit, as does Dr. Ray, that it is difficult to disentangle oneself from the prejudices of one's childhood, but they feel that they are making genuine headway.

"They just don't understand," says Willie Cager, one of the 1967-1968 basketball team's co-captains, shaking his head sadly. "Prejudice is prejudice. Either you've got it or you ain't. They got it."

"A single drop of prejudice poisons a man," said the militant Harry Edwards in a recent speech on the UTEP campus. "A Negro who encounters a single act of discrimination seals off his mind."

Another UTEP co-captain, Willie Worsley, keeps a Countee Cullen poem handy to make the point:

> *Once riding in old Baltimore*
> *Heart-filled, head-filled with glee,*
> *I saw a Baltimorean*
> *Keep looking straight at me.*

Now I was eight and very small,
And he was no whit bigger,
And so I smiled, but he poked out
His tongue, and called me, "Nigger."

I saw the whole of Baltimore
From May until December;
Of all the things that happened there
That's all that I remember.

The University of Texas at El Paso is a bad place for a black man, but it is not easy to tell where the prejudice originates. The athletic department and the coaches explain certain acts of prejudice, such as clamping down on Negroes who date white girls, in terms of the El Paso business community. "El Paso isn't ready for interracial dating," the coaches warn their black athletes. But when one seeks an explanation from El Paso businessmen, one is told that it makes no difference to them whom the Negroes date, so long as the school wins a few ball games now and then. One wonders if UTEP is following the town's prejudices or the town is following the school's. Whichever, it is immaterial to the 40 or 50 black scholarship athletes. Almost unanimously, they regard the place as a ghetto. "We were suckered into coming here," says Willie Cager. "I come from the toughest, blackest, poorest part of the Bronx. I won't be unhappy to go back."

All the standard methods of dealing with black athletes are used at UTEP, and in sum they add up to the same old story: the black athlete is there to perform, not to get an education, and when he has used up his eligibility, he is out. "The coaches say that education is the important thing and sports comes second," says Willie Cager, "but you soon learn better. They want you to *win* first. All the sports requirements—practice, schedules, road trips—come first."

Dave Lattin was one of the seven Negroes who were starters or top substitutes on the 1966 championship basketball team. Like the others, he lacks a degree from UTEP. According to Lattin, "If you played basketball, you spent most of your time in the gym, on and off season. You didn't get a chance to spend much time studying. So you'd drop behind your classmates. The only way you could stay in the ball game was to kind of lighten up on your courses. You really had to blow your neck to do the right thing, to go to class every day and go to practice every day and study after practice. Basketball would average out to about forty hours a week, and we practiced seven days a week. During the season we got *no* days off. It was just like a job. It's easier in the pros."

To maintain such a schedule and stay eligible, the Negro athlete could take certain steps. "You could switch to Mickey Mouse courses, where you don't work too hard," says Willie Cager. "I had to keep taking courses like music and art, and now I'm a senior and I'm twenty-one hours short of graduation. And the worst part of it is that the courses I have to make up are things like biology and kinesiology, that I have to have for a degree in physical education."

Certain "friendly" professors can be counted on to assist the athlete, black or white. Willie Worsley speaks highly of a teacher "who understands the problems, and he don't embarrass anybody, illiterate or not. Somebody told him that Negro athletes needed help in their grades and we are all making Bs in his class now."

Then there are the professors who can turn difficult courses into snaps. "They give the same tests from year to year," says Dr. John West, head of the English department, "and they never have a new thought. They use the same notes, the same approaches. And tests that are returned are made available, and it would only be natural if some turned up in the athletic area."

Tutors can be helpful too. Says Cager: "If a kid isn't smart enough or has too bad a background, but they need him to play a sport, the tutor sometimes will do his work for him."

Dr. Joseph Ray is not unaware of some of the academic dodges that have gone on at UTEP. But he argues, "The principal thing is that as Negroes their preparation before they came here was not as dependable as it should be." He admits that the university has exploited some of its black athletes, but no more than all universities exploit athletes, black or white. "I can think of one Negro athlete who, they recognized, would not be able to stay eligible if he took all the required courses, and so they *kept* him eligible. Our athletic council took notice that this sort of thing was going on, and it's being terminated. *It's being terminated.* But that happens at a lot of places. We're not the only ones that ever did it."

UTEP is not the only school that ever slipped a little extra financial assistance to its athletes, either; the practice is common and widespread and almost inevitable under stern NCAA rules. "We're supposed to get ten dollars a month plus room and board and tuition and books," says Willie Cager. "Who can live on that? We're all in bad financial shape, but there's no use discussing it. You know yourself that the alumni are always putting up money to help the athletes. What burns us is that somehow it never reaches the black athletes here. We never see that money."

"I'm not asking for money to be slipped to me," says All-America linebacker Fred Carr, the first-round draft choice of the Green Bay Packers. "All I'm saying is that if there's some extra money being provided to help athletes through financial binds, then it should be used by black *and* white. Now I know that some of the white athletes get this kind of help, but the Negroes don't. I'd get a note in my box saying 'Nice game.' I'll buy that; I'm not looking for money. But then, don't give it to the white players!"

"If a Negro looks for help, he doesn't find it," says Bob Beamon, AAU long-jump champion in 1968. "I have a four-year-old car that needs three hundred dollars worth of repairs. I don't know where I'm gonna get the money to fix it. If I were the *white* long-jump champion, that car would be fixed like magic. But me, I'm poor. I'm broke, busted and disgusted."

The problem with the car would not disturb Beamon if he could walk to the campus, "but there's no decent housing for the married Negro anywhere near the school, so my wife and I live two miles away and I have to have that car. So I go around borrowing money, practically *begging* people for money, and I wind up in debt."

"A Negro will be more apt to get in debt here than a white athlete," says Willie Worsley. "I tell you how they'll help a Negro; they'll send him down to Household Finance. In other words, they'll help you get in debt. But with the whites, it's the old story. They'll help them, at least moderately. Now, it wouldn't be so bad if they'd give us more help getting jobs in the summer."

"I went in two months before vacation break to ask McCarty to help me find a job, the way he does with the white players," says former halfback Willie Fields. "He said he didn't know of anything, but I might be able to get a job raking leaves or something like that. But I know white players who asked him to find them a job and he got them jobs the next day at three dollars an hour."

According to the Negroes, their wives are treated the same way. "My wife is a qualified secretary, bilingual in English and Spanish," Beamon says. "They got her a job at a dollar, thirty-five an hour, lifting boxes." Fred Carr tells about a Negro athlete whose wife spent three months looking for a job, with the assistance of the UTEP athletic department. "They were having a hell of a time financially," Carr says, "and we'd lend them what we could. So he finally went to the coach and asked if he could borrow some money and the coach sent him off to a loan company off the campus. He never *did* get the money. And then, in comes a white athlete, a junior-college transfer, and they got his wife a job in three days. They say that the Negro wives can't get jobs because they are not qualified. Well, most of them are."

Acute as money problems sometimes are, they are not as deeply painful as the chronic emptiness of the black athlete-student's life on campus. You can see the Negro students of UTEP almost any day of the week, drinking Cokes and playing cards at the last two tables in the rear of the spa, pool hall and bowling alley in the basement of the Student Union Building. If you could not tell them by their color, you could tell them by their bored look. A high percentage of them are scholarship athletes, "professional amateurs." The university does not seem to have any great interest in other kinds of Negroes, such as scholars. "We made an effort to get some qualified Negroes and give them scholarships," says an administrator, "but we got too much competition from places like Harvard and Yale." But by assiduous recruiting, they get a bounteous supply of black athletes. They arrive nervous but full of enthusiasm, and two weeks later they are slouching about the campus like condemned men in the exercise area.

"They told me that college would be a rewarding experience," says Fred Carr. "They said I'd meet people, I'd travel. Well, I did, but I still call college the time of my greatest suffering. I came from Phoenix, Arizona, where they didn't push Negroes around. And then I came to college and discovered prejudice."

"There is not a thing that goes on here that I like," says Bob Wallace. "We don't have nowhere to go. After every game we are supposed to stay around the dorm playing cards. Nothing to do. *Nothing* to do. And these are supposed to be the best years of our lives. And it turns out to be a drag."

"We can't even get into the fraternities," says Jerri Wisdom. "I was so innocent, I went through a frat rush. One day a guy called me aside and he said, 'Hey man, forget it!' I knew a Jewish kid who was hanging around with some Negro kids and the guys in the fraternity he had pledged told him to cut it out. That's before they found out he was Jewish. Then they dropped him altogether. They told him to go find a Jewish fraternity. Me, I was so dumb I kept trying to get in, but I didn't make it."

Jimmy Walker, the conscientious dean of students, says, "I asked Kelly Myrick, one of our scholarship Negroes, just what's the problem. He said, 'Not being accepted.' Well, don't tell *them* this, but this is a problem that's gonna take a while to solve! But don't say 'Wait!' to these people, because they're not interested. They cut you off, and I don't know that I blame them. It's how people look at them. How people look! What are you gonna do? Can we go out and give our white students orders, 'Now when the Negroes come by, you look *this* way?' The complaints are valid, but it's a son of a gun to do anything about."

Not even the black heroes of the 1966 championship basketball team were spared the "looks," the double standard that is visited upon Negroes. "After that 1966 game in College Park, Maryland," says Willie Worsley, "we came back to the campus and there were two thousand people waiting for us at the airport. They paraded us through town and everybody was going crazy, cheering and hollering, and then somebody had the team to a banquet and we all ate steak. But that was about the end of it. We were never campus heroes. We were never invited to mixers or anything like that. If there was a banquet for the team, it was always kept to the team. When we won that game in 1966, there wasn't more than fifty Negroes on the campus, and most were athletes from out of town. But we was animals. The whites call the Negro football players cannibals and the basketball players animals. You play basketball and that's it. When the game's over they want you to come back to the dormitory and stay out of sight."

Says Willie Cager: "People don't stand up and holler 'nigger' at you, but it's just as bad. You know that when you finish playing the game, if you played a good game you're gonna get a pat on the back, more or less like a dog, and then they put you to sleep, and if you play a bad game you're still gonna get sent to your house for the night and then they're gonna talk about how lousy you were. The people here don't come right out and say that they hate your guts and all you can do is play basketball and nothing else, but that is how it shapes up."

Among the school's black football players there were two who translated their sense of grievance into action as long ago as 1965. When Fred Carr joined the team, he and a teammate, Eugene Jackson (now of the Cleveland Browns), became so discouraged that they just left school. Coach Bobby Dobbs had to enlist the assistance of the Arizona Highway Patrol to get them back. Carr remembers it as a scene from an old movie:

"At that time, the white guys on the team didn't have the ability of the guys on my high-school team. And the prejudice was pitiful. Plus the fact that I was dating a white girl back home in Phoenix and the football players found out about it. I had my girl's picture on my desk in the dorm, and the white players would come in and stand there and stare at it. One day Coach Dobbs took me aside and told me, 'There's too many girls in the world to be worried about one.' Somebody else in the athletic department told me I was a potential outrage to the El Paso community. If I dated a white girl back home, then I might start dating white girls here. So Eugene Jackson and I talked to one of the assistant football coaches about the whole situation, and he said, 'Look, when you're on the field you're my property, but when you're off the field you can do anything you want.' That was all right with us, but we found out that Coach Dobbs didn't feel the same way. This was his empire. He wasn't gonna let us mess up his world.

"So we were having two-a-day practices and me and Eugene packed up and headed for the Arizona line. The man stopped us at the inspection station at the border and he said, 'What's your name?' We told him and he said, 'You guys wait here, the highway patrolman will be here in a minute.' So the highway patrolman came over and said he had a phone call for us to make. We called the number and it was Bobby Dobbs and he talked us into coming back. He laughed about it, and he said, 'If you come back I won't hold no hard feelings; I'll never bring it up no more.'"

Dobbs's version of the story differs in slight detail. "Carr had just come to a new school, and this incident had nothing to do with the racial issue. We have any number of kids who come here and get lonesome. This terrain is right in the desert, and if they come from a different part of the country, it takes 'em a little while to get adjusted. Fred had only been here a couple of days, and he and this big end, Eugene Jackson, left. The Arizona papers wrote a story that we called the police and made 'em come back. That's hogwash. All we did was ask the police to just tell the boys to call us. They had left without talking to us and they were back that night. The reason we did it is because we can't afford to lose athletes like that."

Dobbs got his players back, but nothing was permanently settled; revolt was now in the air—and spreading in the wind. One Wednesday early in the 1967 football season, the team was scheduled to attend a scouting-report meeting, but the Negro members staged a sit-in in the lobby of the athletic dormitory. Dobbs, a former assistant coach at West Point, hurried over to see what was going on, and was met by a solid wall of black dissent and complaint. Every black member of the team was there, and All-Americas Fred Carr and Charlie West were among the leaders. Says Carr: "We told him that we wanted to date whoever we wanted to, because there weren't any Negro girls to date, and we asked him to use his influence to get some Negro girls on the campus. We told him we knew he could go to some people downtown and tell them to arrange scholarships for Negro girls. His word would swing it. Give 'em music scholarships, anything. There are plenty of deserving Negro girls around. Why do all the scholarship Negroes have to be athletes? We told him about the wives' situation, that Leroy Johnson's wife, who was trained as a private secretary, was running off mimeograph papers for forty dollars a week while Billy Stevens' [the team's white quarterback] wife and all them was making three hundred, four hundred a month and Billy still drawing seventy-two dollars a month from the school. We told him we didn't like the way he and his coaches treat people on the field—making Negroes the butt of jokes, kicking them around and treating them bad. We told him the food was spoiled, but everybody complains about that. We told him nobody was cleaning up the rooms of the Negro athletes. We had to do our own. There was a Mexican maid assigned up there, but she wouldn't come to the Negro rooms but once a month, and she was doing the white guys' rooms three or four times a week.

"We tried to hit him right where it counted. In the wallet. We told him we were ready to walk out, and he knew it. So when it was all over, he said that we should have come to see him in a committee, not mobbed all over him like this. He said he would do his level best to see what he could do about our complaints. And he said he thought we should keep this among ourselves. We agreed not to tell the papers or nobody— that was a mistake.

"So the upshot of the whole thing was nothing. Not a single thing happened. And a little while later we began to hear rumbles that they were going to stop recruiting Negroes. One member of the athletic department made the statement that from now on the only Negroes they'd recruit would be stars like O. J. Simpson. He said they were through with the soso Negro athletes, they used up too much of the grub and they caused too much trouble. And it wasn't very long before the whole way they recruit here had seemed to change.

"Instead of seeing nothing but Negro kids coming in to look around the campus, all of a sudden you began seeing a lot of white kids. So I think they are cutting down on the Negroes. I guess that's what we get for our sit-in."

Bobby Dobbs discusses the affair with the air of a man probing his memory for the details of something that happened eons ago and was not terribly significant anyway. "Yes," he says, "they aired a few complaints. Food was one of them, and certainly I listened to them. They asked for a few things to improve their living conditions and certainly I listened to them. . . . And they asked me to use my influence to bring some Negro girls here on scholarship. That's a common complaint on campuses. But it's difficult to alter. One thing I did apologize for: I had made a remark to the team one day to the effect that 'we're all free, white and twenty-one,' and then I realized what I had said and I added quickly, 'some of us!' I didn't mean that as a racial remark at all; it's just one of those things that pop out, and I told them I was sorry about that, very sorry."

When open rebellion finally confronted UTEP's athletic department, it came from an unexpected direction. There was a time when the black members of UTEP's track team were considered the original good guys around the campus. Let the football team gripe and complain like a bunch of children; let the basketball players lament about how they were being treated like animals instead of the ebony gods that they thought they were; one could always depend on fellows like Bob Beamon, the champion long-jumper, and Dave Morgan, the feisty ex-Marine quarter-miler, and all the other blacks on the squad. The track team was *together*, one solid unit. Under the direction of coach Wayne Vandenburg the Miners had an outside chance to become NCAA champions, if not in 1968, then certainly in 1969. The track squad was the pride of El Paso. Because of it, the once unknown school now had its second shot at a national championship in three years.

The high point of this interracial cinder romance came when the UTEP track team hied itself off to New York's Madison Square Garden in 1968 for the annual New York Athletic Club track meet. A big boycott was on, the point of which was simple: The NYAC does not admit Negroes to its membership, but each year it makes a potful of money by exhibiting star Negroes at its track meet; why should Negro amateur athletes perform for such a left-handed cause?

When word got out that the UTEP blacks would defy the boycott and compete, other black athletes tightened down on them. There were threatening phone calls. Harry Edwards announced that the team members would get to New York, see the picket line, and quit. Otherwise, said Edwards, he could not be responsible for anything that happened to them. Rap Brown, then chairman of the Student Nonviolent Coordinating Committee, announced that Madison Square Garden ought to be blown up. "My boys were scared to death," says Coach Vandenburg. "I said to each one, 'Listen, you don't have to go through with this.' "

Why did they?

Bob Beamon says the Negro trackmen had long meetings and discussed the situation thoroughly. "It got down to this," he says. "The NYAC is prejudiced against a lot of different kinds of people, including Jews, and if they're that way, why should we get excited about it? What happens if we boycott and they agree to admit Negroes but they still keep out the Jews? What have we accomplished?"

If the logic is tortured, it is possibly because it conceals a more basic reason why the Negroes voted to compete. Most of them are from the Northeast. Star quarter-miler Dave Morgan is from Norristown, Pennsylvania. Beamon is from Jamaica, New York. Jose L'Official is from New York, and so are several others. "Okay, let's admit it," says Beamon. "Most of us hadn't been home for a long time, and we were miserable in El Paso, and here was a chance to visit our people with all expenses paid."

There was a final reason to attend, and pugnacious Dave Morgan explained it: "People like Harry Edwards were telling us we *couldn't* go to the NYAC meet. He was announcing that we would be a bunch of Uncle

Toms and house niggers if we went, and something would happen to us. Well, I spent five years in the Marines and I don't like that kind of talk. Who the hell is Harry Edwards to tell us where we can go and what we can want, what we can do, and what we can't? That teed us off, and if there was ever any chance that we would boycott, it was lost when Edwards started popping off."

The black athletes of UTEP passed through the picket lines and performed under intense pressure from Negro militants. Their performances were understandably lackluster. But when they returned to El Paso, they were the heroes of the campus. They were the Negroes who had stood up to the militants. They were "our boys." Says Dave Morgan: "We got a pat on the back, a pat on the head. 'Great job, wonderful!' 'You really stood up for your rights.' 'Good job, black boy,' that's what they were really saying. After about two hours of all this praise and backslapping, we were sent back to our pigeonholes and our roles as niggers."

But the New York trip started the Negroes thinking. Bob Beamon, an introverted and melancholy young man who is tasting his first severe racial prejudice in El Paso, began engaging in long discussions with Dave Morgan and a few of the other black trackmen, after the NYAC meet. Morgan had come to his own decision quickly: that a stand would have to be made against some of the practices at UTEP. But Beamon, the other natural leader of the black runners and jumpers, continued to vacillate. He acted like a man who could not understand what was happening around him, like a man who stands in front of a truck and cannot assimilate the fact that it is bearing down on him. He would blurt

66

out naïve questions like: "Can you explain something to me: How can people hate each other?" and "Why is it that white people are so prejudiced against colored people?" He would sit around and write poems addressed to the white race:

> How many days of sadness must I spend
> To get hatred into gladness?
> And tell me how much sorrow must I spend
> To get a future for tomorrow?
> This must be a proud nation of crudeness.
> This world used to mean so very much.
> Why did you change my happiness to misery and heartbreak?
> How must I be lonely?
> Why can't you love me and want me
> Until the end of time?

Then came the assassination of Martin Luther King. It ended all the wool-gathering and brooding and it brought the Negro trackmen into a cohesive unit. At the request of their coach, they competed in the Texas Relays the week-end following the assassination. As half-miler John Nichols of Watts, California, said later: "We were upset, most of us. We went to the coach and told him we didn't feel like running, and he said, 'I know how you feel, I feel just as bad as you do, but get out there and run!' So we all ran, even though our hearts weren't even there. The coach patted us on the behinds and said, 'Go out there and do it! You can do it!' Well we did it, but we were pretty lousy."

When they returned to El Paso they saw Harry Edwards very briefly as he was leaving, but his influence on their actions was not nearly as great as UTEP authorities would like to believe. As soon as they got back to the campus the Negro trackmen held a secret meeting. Next on the schedule was an Easter week track meet against Utah State and Brigham Young University, at Provo, Utah. BYU is a Mormon school, and the Book of Mormon specifies an inferior role for Negroes. Most of the blacks decided to beg off the track meet. "There were about a dozen reasons," says Dave Morgan. "The Mormons teach that Negroes are descended from the Devil. No Negro can become an officer of the Mormon Church. As a reason for the track team's boycott, it may sound like a small thing to a white person, but who the hell wants to go up there and run your tail off in front of a bunch of spectators that think you've got horns? Martin Luther King was part of it, too. We had never had a chance to show how we felt about his death. Coach Vandenburg had asked us to run at Austin and we ran, when probably the whole meet should have been cancelled, out of respect to Dr. King. We still felt sad about that. And the meet at BYU was in Easter week, and it seemed to us that there was an obvious connection between the martyrdom of Jesus and the martyrdom of Dr. King. To a white, it might be nothing; to us it had great significance. And on top of all of that, there was the general fact that the Negro is treated like something out of the jungle here and we wanted to express ourselves about that."

On the Monday night before the meet with Brigham Young, nine Negro trackmen arrived at the small apartment of Coach Vandenburg and presented their grievances. According to the young and outspoken coach: "They mentioned all kinds of crazy things. They said Beamon's wife should have a better job. They talked about the Mormon Church and they talked about the lack of jobs in El Paso and the unfair housing. I said,

'Fellows, let's get to the point! Man, you're keeping me up all night!' But there *was* no point! Nothing! When they left, about eleven-thirty, I felt that everything was settled. But ten minutes later there's a knock on my door and it's Kelly Myrick, the hurdler. He says, 'We're boycotting.' I said, 'Who are you speaking for?' He said, 'The whole nine who were in the room.' "

On Tuesday and Wednesday the recalcitrant athletes showed up at track practice, and Vandenburg began to entertain hope that the boycott was off. When he heard informally that the athletes were going to refuse to head for Utah, he prepared a statement saying that they were, in effect, quitting the team. Seven of the Negroes issued a statement of their own:

TELLING IT LIKE IT IS

We, the University of Texas at El Paso trackmen, would like to issue the following statement concerning the BYU-Utah State track meet:

First, in correlation to participating in the Texas Relays, we the Black athletes feel that the coach should have been more sympathetic toward us, the Black athletes, concerning our feelings toward the assassination of Dr. Martin Luther King. This does not mean we will not participate in any future meets if permitted.

Since this is a Holy Week, a Holy cause for all Blacks, we feel our participating should not include the BYU meet for this coming weekend, because of their beliefs that the Blacks are inferior and that we are disciples of the devil.

As athletes we feel that our coach did not use his formal authority in reference to our present situation. The open public announcement made by Wayne Vandenburg, "Any of my athletes that do not participate in the upcoming meet with BYU

69

will be dropped from the team." Quote: Unquote:

Also, we feel that the coach is forcing us into a corner with his above statement of dropping us from the team, when we feel we have a just reason for not participating in the meet.

This statement is specific, but all aspects of it will be simplified and told exactly like it is in the near future.

On Thursday night, assistant athletic director Jim Bowden talked to the boycotting athletes for three hours. According to school president Joseph Ray, "Jim told them what would happen if they went through with their plan. He told them that he didn't necessarily disagree with them on principle, but he said they were paying too big a price to make their point." According to the athletes, Bowden told them flatly that they would be off the track squad and lose their scholarships if they refused to go to Utah. After the session with Bowden, Coach Vandenburg asked the Negroes if they wanted to have another talk with him. They said they had done all their talking. The track team left—eight Negroes remained in El Paso. At Provo the team was joined by Negro half-miler John Nichols, an art major, who was in sympathy with the boycotters but wanted to see for himself the situation at Brigham Young.

"I wanted to boycott," says Nichols. "My heart was with those other guys, but I also couldn't believe that it was so bad up at Utah. So as soon as we got to Provo, I began talking to people. One of my teammates started talking about my buddies back in El Paso, how they had screwed up their lives and now they were blackballed for life, stuff like that. I couldn't understand it— I always thought he was a friend of mine. So I said, 'Hey, brighten up, you're talking about my friends!' So he charges me and calls me 'black boy' and I had to knock him on his ass. I ran out and told the coach,'I can't run. I can't run in this thing.' He looked at me as though I was crazy, and he walked away."

Along with the signers of the original statement, Nichols now became an ex-member of the track team. The press was told that the suspension was for the current school year and that next year's athletic scholarships would be discussed when the time came. But each of the boycotting Negroes claims he was told that his scholarship would terminate at the end of the year; he should look elsewhere. Coach Vandenburg took a reporter aside and said, "They're finished. There's no special rules for blacks and whites or greens and pinks, man. I'm hired to do the best job according to my ability, to decide all these things for everybody, and I *decided*. I didn't kick them off; they quit."

President Ray and the faculty athletic council declined to veto Vandenburg's action. "If there is a case of compassion," Dr. Ray said, "it would be up to the coach. Nobody's gonna tell him what to do. I regret this very much. These are good boys. But they either collectively or individually hoodwinked themselves into the conviction that we wouldn't let them all go. A whole lot of pushing has been done by Negroes, and that pushing is going to hasten the day when your Negro comes close to equality. But I think in this case they paid a hell of a price to win their point. . . .This is a price that no college athletes in this country have ever yet paid for a point on this issue. They were laying down their collegiate athletic lives and they surely knew it. The pressure that Negro activists are applying in this country is tolerable only under terms of the application of standard rules. A man who's in a store looting it has either got to be arrested or if he runs, he's got to be shot down. They've got to function within the rules. Otherwise we don't have a society; we've got mob rule. . . ."

The black athletes' difficulties did not end with the lifting of athletic scholarships. Bob Beamon's wife had a decent job at last (Vandenburg reportedly found it for her within an hour when it was raised as a boycott issue the Monday before the meet at Provo), and on the Monday morning after the meet she started off to her first day of work. Beamon drove her to the office and went back home for 40 winks. The phone woke him up. "Bob?" his wife said. "You better come get me." He hurried back and picked her up. She told him that her new boss had taken her aside and said that he understood Beamon was no longer affiliated with UTEP. "I told him you were still at the school," Mrs. Beamon said, "and he told me, 'Look, I can't get involved in this thing. You can't have the job.' "

That afternoon an officer of a bank called Beamon and said, "Bob, I heard that you lost your scholarship. Will you be able to pay your bills?" Beamon told the banker that he had not lost his scholarship yet and he would be able to pay his bills, but several other callers asked the same question. "I don't know," Beamon says. "Was it pressure? I don't know. But I do know that the whole town was against us. The whole town lined up with Wayne Vandenburg."

"We are alone in this thing," John Nichols said. "One reason is the papers. As usual they distort the facts against us. Look at this." He produced a two-column newspaper story on the boycott. In a thousand words or so the article described the events that led

72

up to the boycott, but it omitted the vital point: the feeling on the part of the blacks that was aroused by the fact that Mormons teach the inferiority of Negroes. Thus the Negro argument was made to look petty and capricious.

"For some reason," Dave Morgan said, "this newspaper decided that it didn't want to tell the people why we're boycotting, so it just substituted a little old point that they made up out of thin air. That's what passes for reporting, and that's why nobody has the slightest sympathy for us. They read the papers and they think we're just plain nuts."

Morgan emerged as the acknowledged leader of the rebellious Negroes, and the role was a strange one for him. "Up until now the coaches used to use me as a mediator," he says. "I'm older, I was in the Marine Corps, I've got good grades. The athletic department used me as an Uncle Tom, and every time there was a racial incident the coaches would run and get me. Well, they won't run and get me anymore. I was the athletic department's boy as long as I would go along with what they said and let them pat me on the head and call me 'boy.' As long as I let them do the thinking for me. But the minute I want to do something and think for myself a little, they ridicule me and say that I'm somebody's misguided child, that Harry Edwards was behind all this. Well, let me tell you something: Harry Edwards was behind *nothing*. He came to this campus and tried to stir the Negroes up. But he didn't have the slightest effect on us. Now you hear all over the campus that Harry Edwards wrote the statement we handed out about our position. You want to know who wrote that statement? I wrote it! *Dave Morgan wrote it!* Harry Edwards has not and will not sway my position in any way whatsoever! I'm not a little child that has to be led by Harry Edwards. And neither is anybody else involved in this thing."

As for 1968, the disbarred Negro trackmen said they would show up on the campus at registration time, just like the other undergraduates. "We're gonna lay our eighty-seven dollars on the table," Beamon says, "and register for class. That's the fee for residents of the state of Texas, and we're gonna say, 'Here we are, we Texans, and we're paying our own way.' " (The plan has a flaw: most of them probably cannot qualify as Texas residents.)

"We're not gonna run away from what's being shoved in our face here," says Nichols. "We'll scrape, scrounge and borrow, but we're coming back to finish our educations. Next year at registration time, they're gonna find out damn fast who the house niggers are!"

As for Coach Vandenburg, he remained inflexible on the subject, but one can see that underneath he has been shattered by what has happened. Vandenburg is an ambitious young man from Cicero, Illinois, and he works harder than any of his runners to bring athletic recognition to the University of Texas at El Paso. In his second year on the campus, he was all primed to win the National championship. "Look what happened," he says. "Look what this thing did to the track team. We lost the world indoor record holder in the long jump, the school record holder in the hurdle, the school record holder in the quarter mile, the freshman hurdle champion, a couple of outstanding intermediate runners, a fine long-jump and triple-jump man—and *not one of them seniors*. Of those we lost in all, four were soph-

74

omores, three were juniors and two were freshmen. It hurts, sure it does. We had aspirations of winning the NCAA championship this year. At least we'd have been second or third. *Track and Field News* picked us third, three points behind second place. Now we're not gonna win anything except maybe a few dual meets. It kills us. We've lost almost every Negro on the squad."

Wayne Vandenburg, himself only four or five years older than most of his athletes, squared his shoulders and raised his voice. "Okay, it's over now!" he said. "But next year's another year. We're still gonna be strong next year. I came in here fast and I'm gonna keep on going."

So are the Negroes.

"Oh, I Can Read, but
It's Such a Burden": Learning
the White Man's Language

4

Certain truths about the Negro college athlete have been carefully concealed, and for good reason. Some of the truths are painful; some are embarrassing; some show too clearly the heavy hand of white America. The most obvious of these truths is that precious few Negro athletes are qualified to attend college in the first place. The gulf between the secondary schools of the white and those of Negroes remains a Grand Canyon; few of the Negro athletes who arrive on college campuses have ever read a book from cover to cover, or had any reason to. They were too busy facing cockroaches, rats, hunger, crime and all the other problems that bedevil the poor. Arriving on campus, they wallow in fear and confusion as they confront seemingly insurmountable academic challenges.

A good example is Jo Jo White, a senior at the University of Kansas, an All-America basketball player, and perhaps the key man on the U.S. Olympic basketball team. He is a markedly handsome man of light-brown color, sad brown eyes and a close-cropped head of hair that fits neatly around his skull like an oversized *yarmulke.* When strange whites are around, he talks almost in a mumble barely audible. He comes from the ghetto section of St. Louis, but he attended an integrated high school. Intelligence tests show him to be slightly above average, on a level with thousands of white students at the University of Kansas.

But All-America Jo Jo White has a terrible time reading. "Oh, I can read," he says, "but it's such a burden that I just don't do it. If I have to, I can read and comprehend a book. But just to sit down and read one because I want to—that's something I never do. Like if somebody hands me a book and says, 'This is a good book, you ought to read it,' why, he's giving me *work* to do, not any pleasure."

Jo Jo White has finished four years at Kansas, but he did not graduate in 1968. KU requires three basic English courses from its graduates; most students polish them off in the first few semesters. Jo Jo has tried and tried, but he has not been able to pass the simplest of the three courses. When the pressure of basketball has lifted from him, he will try again. But if Jo Jo White is like most other Negroes in American colleges, he will finally give up and drop out of school, minus diploma.

John Novotny, the athletic counselor at the University of Kansas entertains no illusions about the extent of this cultural gulf. "You go to their houses and there's not a single book," Novotny says. "People forget: it's a *white* pastime to have a bookshelf. You look around a Negro household and you don't see a book, not even on a table somewhere. White people can't seem to realize the environments these boys come from. It's easier to sit back and say they're inherently stupid, racially inferior, than it is to confront this problem and see it whole, and *do something about it*. You should see the applications we get from Negro athletes. Under Parents' Education they put down fourth grade, seventh grade, in very rare cases ninth or tenth grade. That's the extent of it. And that usually means a low grade in a predominantly Negro school, where the standards are almost always lower. But it's interesting: most of the applications we get are very carefully filled out, neatly written, perfectly spelled. Why? Because they're filled out by somebody else. The athlete can't trust himself to get it right."

Few Negroes are willing to discuss the cultural gulf; they prefer to pretend that it does not exist. The Negro has been called stupid for so many generations that he is supersensitive about allusions to such matters as his reading speed, his spelling, his cultural background. Don Shanklin is one of the rare Negroes who face up to the intellectual limitations imposed on them from childhood. "No, I never read a book till I came to college. I been working since I was twelve. When was I gonna read? And besides that, there wasn't anything to read around our house."

Harry Gunner, now with the Cincinnati Bengals, had read one book before entering college: *The Willie Mays Story*. Willie McDaniel of KU cannot recall reading a real book, "But I did read some comic books. No, come to think of it I mostly just looked at the pictures." Melvin Rogers, Elvin Hayes's basketball coach, graduated from an all-Negro high school and an all-Negro college (Southern University) and only then found out that his reading skills were inferior. "I went to LSU for some advanced work, and they expected me to read something like fourteen books in a course, and I found out I couldn't do it. I could read a book in a few days, but those white kids from St. Louis and Texas and places like that got far ahead of me."

The simple fact is that the black athlete who enters a white college must cram his belated education into four hectic years. He must make up for black schools that are underfinanced, understaffed and markedly inferior, and he must excel on the playing field all the while.

Shanklin talks about his "separate-but-equal" high school in Amarillo: "We had all the titles. We had a Spanish teacher, a trig and algebra and geometry teacher, a physics teacher, all the titles. But the trig teacher couldn't teach trig. She didn't have the background. There was a boy in my class used to get up and teach it sometimes; he was supposed to be helping the teacher but he wound up doing more teaching than she did. She'd show us the wrong way to solve a problem, and then this kid would get up and show us how to do it with half as many steps. In English it was the same way, except we didn't have no kid to help out. Maybe we'd mingle around with verbs a little, or study some poems we should have been studying in junior high. In my senior year of English, we wrote one theme. It was the only writing I ever did before I came to college. My theme was on 'What Christmas Means to Me.' Mostly I emphasized the toys and the holiday from school."

Mike Garrett has bad memories of his first days on the campus of the University of Southern California. "I was prepared only for football. I simply couldn't read and write as well as my classmates. How could I compete with students who had gone to high school in Beverly Hills, places like that?"

Percy Harris, who played scholarship football at several southwestern colleges before becoming a football coach at Du Sable High School in Chicago, talks of the shock of entering a white college. "I had no study habits. My English was bad, spelling was bad, reading, *everything* was bad. I don't know *what* I had learned in high school in Chicago. Most of my education had to come in college. That's why it was so tough."

"Secondary education," as whites know it, is a mirage for most Negroes. At Eula D. Britton School, where Elvin Hayes's sister Christine teaches English, a patient and intelligent principal, James Smith, makes the best of what is available to him. "We couldn't offer a foreign language until last year," says Coach Melvin Rogers, "but then they let us bring in a French teacher. Until now, our students were cut way down on their choice of colleges, because most colleges won't accept a high-school graduate with less than two years of a foreign language. So right away we're inadequate. We still don't teach trig or any of the higher math that kids need these days. And we lack facilities. Even when we do get proper facilities, something seems to go wrong. Like, we got a library from a federal grant, and they built the library between the band room and the lunch room. Now you don't have to know anything about education to avoid a mistake like that. You could have closed your eyes and dropped that library in a better place. But who cares? We're an all-Negro school. A library next to the bass drums is good enough for us."

The Northern ghetto schools are not much better. "The differences are almost negligible," says educator Novotny. "About the only advantage the Northern Negro gets is more up-to-date textbooks. He usually gets the same textbooks as the white students, and this isn't always true in the South. Until a few years ago, they had an interesting system in Houston, Texas. When new textbooks came in, say in chemistry, they would go to the white schools; the old chemistry books would be collected and sent to the Negro schools. If the sixth edition of a textbook came out, the fifth edition would be sent to the Negro schools. Houston doesn't do that anymore, but it's still a common practice in parts of the South."

Such practices help to perpetuate the gulf between Negro and white students, which shows up even when it is least expected. One talks to an intelligent Negro athlete who is a few months away from receiving a master's degree. Every hour of his education has been in all-Negro schools. "I started back in 1953," he says. "That was—let me see—" he pauses. "Let's see, this is 1968, that was 1953, so that was—er, ah—yes, fifteen years ago." While he goes through this painful figuring, you want to pipe up, "Fifteen is correct," but do you hand him the answer and risk hurting his pride, or do you let him stumble around and reveal his own arithmetical deficiencies?

The University of Missouri's conscientious football coach, Dan Devine, one of the few coaches with a real understanding of the Negro student-athlete's problems, puts it briefly: "I still get letters from Negro athletes in which such simple things as spelling and punctuation are so bad it makes you want to cry."

Indeed, the biggest part of the Negro college athlete's problem is the English language, spoken one way in the white culture and another in the black. White students, even the least intelligent, develop something of a feel for correct usage, but the most intelligent Negro students arrive on campus talking another tongue; they cannot have a feel for the white man's English because they have seldom heard it spoken.

Morgan Wootten, who coaches basketball at DeMatha Catholic High School in Hyattsville, Maryland, the only high school that ever beat Lew Alcindor's team, remembers asking a white student 10 English questions from the college boards. The boy got all 10 right, but he could not offer the slightest explanation for any of his answers. They just "sounded" right, and since the boy was a white Anglo-Saxon and the college-board examinations have a white, Anglo-Saxon background, the boy scored 100 per cent. When the same 10 questions were asked of Negro students, they would seldom get more than five or six correct.

"Black English has a different vocabulary," says John Novotny. "The average Negro doesn't speak English at home. We should offer him English as a foreign language in college. Sometimes history or political science professors will call me in and show me papers by our Negro athletes, and the expressive ability and the vocabulary are so bad that it just comes out garbled, unbelievable. I saw a paper last semester in a survey course in American history, and the boy was called on to analyze three books of the high school level, and the mess he got himself into, the garbled passages and the obvious plagiarism, were pathetic. He didn't even know how to plagiarize! He couldn't copy correctly from one page to another! That's not stupidity. It's simply lack of background. The problem begins the second the professor gives the assignment. Many of our Negro athletes have never been required to follow instructions. So the first thing that happens is they fail to take down the correct instructions. They don't even hear or comprehend correctly. It's the white man's language, and they aren't getting it."

Dr. John West, head of the English department at the University of Texas at El Paso, says, "There's a much bigger difference between what a white student brings to college and what a black student brings to college than anybody ever imagines. They come into college

82

with four strikes against them. All the professor can do is try to reach them. I have a big survey course in English literature, more than one hundred students, and some of them are Negro athletes. When I come to a big word, I work at paraphrasing, trying to define without insulting, by restating what I've just said in smaller words. I'll say that a person's 'introverted,' and then I'll go on and say, 'He's turned inside, he's not an outgoing sort of guy, he sits around and thinks all the time,' and then I continue as though I hadn't defined 'introverted,' because I don't like to insult them."

The word "negress" popped up in one of Faulkner's short stories in an English Lit course, and a black athlete raised his hand to ask what it meant. The professor explained that "negress" was an archaic feminine usage, like "aviatrix," and the athlete said, "Well, I've been one all my life and I've never heard that word." The class began to guffaw, and the athlete blurted out, "I mean I've been a *Negro*!" A good time was had by all, except, perhaps, the Negro athlete, who once again had been reminded forcefully of the difference between him and the others.

In the white classroom, the Negro athlete often endures unbearable agonies of alienation and just plain fright. Despite all the findings of biologists and anthropologists, most Negroes are convinced that whites are inherently smarter, that the Negro somehow is deficient in brainpower. Many Negroes are just as prone as certain whites to mistake the cultural gulf for a biological gulf, and they downrate themselves accordingly. "How can I keep up with these cats?" a Negro freshman athlete says. "They're white!"

Says Don Chaney, who went to the University of   83

Houston: "When I was a little kid, right up to college, I thought whites were automatically smarter. I didn't think there was any such thing as a dumb white person. It was hammered into us. Now I know better. Now I know I'm just as equal as anybody else. But sometimes, deep in your heart, it gets to you, the difference. When you're in class and you can't exactly express yourself the way you want to. You may be trying to make a nice point, but you don't know how to get around to it. You don't have the words. You understand it yourself, but you can't bring it out. Maybe in a Negro school they'd understand, but now you have whites all around you and you put it in a Negro way and they can't understand what you're saying and they look down on you and they say, 'Well, he don't know what he's talking about,' and you look around and everybody's kinda looking over you. And *you* know you're not dumb, and you know what you're thinking, but do *they* know? So you sit down and be embarrassed."

Says Don Shanklin of the University of Kansas: "When I first went to class, I was a nervous wreck. I would hate for an instructor to call on me. I felt small. I knew that some things had been left out of my schooling. I wasn't up to par with the white students. And I'd say something and it might sound reasonable to me, but it would sound stupid to them. So I just kept my mouth shut and listened."

Says Harry Gunner: "It was hard, so hard. There was such a difference. When I first went to junior college, I had to push myself something awful. There were weeks when I didn't go out of my room, except to eat and use the bathroom. That was the only way I could keep up with the white kids, and even then, I

84

like to flunked out. And when I left junior college for Oregon State it was the same thing all over, and I almost blew the coop again; but I had to make it. I couldn't go home."

Gunner and Shanklin and Chaney are possessed of stiff backbones and an ability to apply the seat of the pants to the seat of the chair and sit up until all hours of the night studying. Other Negro athletes find they simply cannot keep up; they slowly withdraw from campus life and hang around until they have exhausted the last course in art appreciation and the last indulgent professor and the last tutor willing to help them cheat.

"The saddest cases of all are the ones that· could pass but just can't believe it," says John Novotny of KU. "They are so bowled over by the white kids and the big words and the academic atmosphere that they give up. We have Negro kids who will cut a class because they're convinced they'll flunk the test that day. They have an ingrained feeling that they're not going to be successful, so they'll cut. And then I'll get a call from the professor and he'll say, 'Why, that fellow could have passed this test.' A Negro student spends his whole lifetime fighting against a natural feeling ingrained in grammar and high school that he can't compete academically against the white boy."

Although it is possible to remain on the black side of the gulf and still get a college degree, it is more common for the Negro athlete simply to fail to graduate.

So long as he has any eligibility left, he somehow manages to hang on in school. When his eligibility runs out, so does his academic luck. After the last game, his adviser will call him in and say something to the effect that it certainly has been rewarding having him on campus to shoot all those jump shots and run back all those punts, but now it appears that college has served its purpose and the athlete might as well face the fact that he lacks too many credits, too many required courses, to graduate. Of course, if he would like to return next year, at his own expense. . . .

The statistics are depressing. For example, at the University of Washington, between 1957 and 1967, seven Negro football players graduated, 13 did not. At the University of Oregon in the last three years, six Negro athletes graduated, five did not. Of 46 Negro athletes who have attended the University of Utah, only one has finished school in the normal four-year span, and only 11 others eventually got a degree. Utah State has graduated nine of 40 Negro athletes, five of them as four-year students. (In every instance at both Utah schools the ones who returned for degrees were professional football players.) Wyoming officials report they graduate less that 20 per cent of their black athletes. Since 1960, California at Berkeley has graduated seven of 12 football players. Minnesota graduated four of nine Negro athletes in 1966 and 1967, and Michigan State eight of 14 football players in a three-year span. So it goes.

Doug Wardlaw of New Haven came up nine semester hours short at Loyola of Chicago. He could have made up the hours at summer school, but he did not know where the money would come from. "I'm short because it's too hard to take a full schedule when you're on the team," the black sociology major says. "You know, the traveling and the practice. You get too far behind. I think they should pay my way. It's because of their athletic program that I can't finish up."

At that, Doug Wardlaw is much closer to a degree

than many Negro athletes ever get. As Sandy Green of UCLA's football team says, "All the athletic department wants to do is use you. If you let them handle your academic program, you will never graduate. They'll have you in and out of basket weaving and art and tell you that you're fulfilling your requirements."

"They don't get an education, because their primary purpose is to compete," Harry Edwards says of Negro college athletes. "Their primary responsibility is to the athletic department, and at the end of four years they wind up with no degree, no job and no references."

Tex Winter, who went from Kansas State to the University of Washington in 1968, is one of the few white coaches willing to approach the subject with any degree of candor, and Winter does not like what he sees. "In basketball, we're getting ourselves into a situation where we go out and look for the exceptional Negro basketball player, and without regard to his background, education, intelligence, morals and character, we bring him into a white college environment with one purpose in mind— to get what we can out of him as a basketball player. The question now has become, can you win without doing that? Many of these boys have no business on a college campus. They have great basketball ability because they have the physical equipment and because for most of them there is little else to do than develop their natural talents by playing basketball most of the time." Winter is not one of those who pontificate about the characteristics "inherent in the race"; he recognizes the social pressures that can knock a Negro on his back and keep him there. But he insists that not every black youth who has been kept in a horizontal position for most of his life is necessarily college material.

Such a Negro will come to school on a full athletic scholarship and look around him at a world as alien as the Sea of Crises on the moon. He has never seen a college before; none of his relatives or friends went to college; none of his teachers talked about it in high school, or steered him toward the right courses. "Most white students are close to someone who has gone to college," says KU's John Novotny, "and they know there is a course pattern you follow to graduate. A Negro athlete doesn't understand course patterns. His parents and brothers and uncles and friends have never been near a college. So he comes in and simply enrolls in courses. He doesn't understand that first you build a broad base and then you begin to work more specifically toward a degree. The first two years in college, the Negro athlete is unconcerned with his diploma, it's not a goal to him. Athletics is more important. And after two years have passed, he is far from the graduation path, and by the time he's a junior he realizes this and by the time he's a senior he knows he's not going to get a degree. So he says, 'What do I care?' "

The University of Kansas is one of the rare institutions that have begun to develop some pride in their academic standards as well as their showing on the scoreboard, and Negro athletes are beginning to get the attention they need in the classrooms of KU. (It was only yesterday that such athletes as Wilt Chamberlain and Wayne Hightower and Gale Sayers and Walt Wesley were dancing their little dance at KU and then moving on, very little the wiser for the experience. None graduated. Jo Jo White, KU's All-America and U.S. Olympic basketball player, was on the same route, but belated steps were taken to lead him toward a degree.)

The University of Kansas made Novotny athletic counselor in 1967, and with the young educator came some new approaches to the black scholarship athlete. Novotny started with the radical assumption that the Negro athlete was *not* the same as the white. Already some startling breakthroughs have been accomplished. Novotny collars the Negro athletes when they are freshmen, limited by Big Eight rules to playing only a few games. "We have a little time then," Novotny says, "and I work with them to make sure that everything they take counts toward graduation, make sure that they stretch out their real tough courses but don't take too many Mickey Mouse courses."

Under Novotny's guidance, KU has set up a tutorial service for athletes, and the Negroes in the athletic program are flocking to it. "At most schools the tutoring is a catch-up operation," Novotny says. "The student falls behind and then with the aid of tutors plays catch up. But here at Kansas we have a full staff of tutors on duty for two hours, Sunday through Thursday nights, in the same building with the athletes. At the moment the problem arises, the athlete can take it to the tutor. Also, certain professors who are interested in athletics got together and set up remedial classes at night, five nights a week, mostly in basic English. These are crash programs aimed at helping the Negro athlete to compete academically right from the beginning. If the Negro student can bring up his English, he can bring up all his marks."

Black athletes who once found themselves ignored in the classrooms at KU are now the beneficiaries of new teaching techniques that help them bridge the black-white gulf. Take the case of Richard Bradshaw, a six-

foot-three-inch guard on the KU basketball team. Bradshaw came out of Chicago's all-black West Side ghetto,
where he had set athletic records at Marshall High
School. But he could hardly talk to a white person. "He
had lived in an all-black world," Novotny says, "and
when he had to talk to a white, he would break out in
a sweat and shake all over."

Bradshaw was a disaster in his freshman public-speaking course. He would get up to make a speech, look out
over the white faces, and almost have to be hauled off
to the campus infirmary. Twice he attempted to talk
on a subject he knew best, basketball, but even on
those familiar grounds he was not able to get off more
than a few garbled words. He began begging off the required speeches and cutting classes, and he wound up
with an "incomplete" in the course. Back he went for a
second semester of public speaking, with the same results. "The teachers just didn't understand the situation
at all," Novotny says. "Everybody has a little stage
fright in public-speaking classes, but this went far beyond stage fright. This was a complete inability to
communicate with anyone white in color."

When Bradshaw doggedly enrolled in the course for
the third consecutive semester, Novotny discussed the
problem with the teacher, Mrs. Shirley Masterson Gilham, and together they worked out an experimental
plan. At first Mrs. Gilham would sit with Bradshaw
and have simple, face-to-face conversations with him.
Later she began meeting him at the university library
and art gallery, and there she would ask his opinions.
"She'd say, 'Rich, what do you think about this painting?'" Novotny recalls, "and little by little his responses
got more and more natural. Soon she began adding a

few white students to the group, and finally she brought Bradshaw to the point where he was able to give a ten-minute talk to the class. He spoke on basketball. His eye contact, his projection were just beautiful. You'd think he'd had a couple of speech courses. He wound up with a B in the course."

The treatment was no cure-all; Bradshaw is still uneasy around whites, and he is still painfully shy and soft-spoken. "But I feel like I might be on the way," he says. "At least I know the barrier is there, and I think I know what I have to do to break through it."

There is a standard argument against such teaching techniques, and Novotny and other educators hear it often. "Why all this special handling of Negroes?" says a fraternity officer at KU. "While Mrs. Gilham is giving this special treatment to Rich Bradshaw, she's neglecting better students." One answer is that Mrs. Gilham and others like her are working on their own time with the special problems of the Negroes. But another white student gives a better answer: "If we're going to recruit deprived Negroes and exploit them in sports, then we've got to give them the special educational treatment they require. If we don't want to give them special attention, we'd better stop recruiting them."

Some few coaches are beginning to understand that the Negro athlete can no longer be drilled in the rudiments of the fast break and then nudged toward the general direction of the classroom without any further assistance. "Every coach that recruits a young man has responsibilities to that player from the moment he steps on campus," says Jim Padgett, the enlightened new head basketball coach at the trouble-torn University of California. "He has to make sure the boy lives through that first 'Dear John' letter from his girl friend, that first test he doesn't pass when he felt he should have passed, all the problems that beset a new student in a new setting. It's a huge step for the Negro athlete, coming to a cosmopolitan university, and his problems are going to be greater, and those problems are the responsibility of the coach who brings him here."

"That was the big lack, the big problem," says Atlanta Falcon Junior Coffey about his playing days at the University of Washington. "Coach [Jim] Owens seemed to feel that just because you're a Negro, he shouldn't give you that extra hand. But that's wrong. A Negro in college is facing a big challenge, and he sometimes gets confused and needs guidance. The whites have all this. They have more businessmen, lawyers, doctors and other whites to turn to. We scarcely have anybody. The feeling towards Negroes seems to be, 'You're on your own.' "

College is an enormous challenge for all students who are recruited for their physical talents rather than their academic skills, and this has been true over the decades for many a white athlete. The fact that the challenge is greater in degree for the black athlete—given his blighted educational background—has not persuaded college recruiters to be more discriminating in their search for star material. The system of communications between high-school and college coaches has simply expanded to include the pursuit of the gifted Negro as well as the star white.

There is a brisk brokerage in hotshot black athletes, and the college athletic directors are the original guys who can't say no. George Gaddy of Detroit is one of the friendly brokers; he specializes in working out arrangements under which intellectually deprived Negro high school boys find their ways to college campuses. Gaddy, a 1941 graduate of Fisk University, teaches physical education at the Moore School in Detroit, and on the side he runs a sports club called "The Collegians." George Gaddy's initiative and enterprise have placed something like a hundred Negro boys in schools of higher education throughout the land. *Should* they be enrolled in schools of higher education? To George Gaddy, the answer is an unqualified "yes." He cannot see how a few extra years in the college environment can fail to help a boy, and he continues to urge his students to excell in sports as a way out of the ghetto.

In his line of work, Gaddy has to have a certain expertise. He explains: "There are different ways to get a boy into college. If he wants to do some studying, he can take a high-school equivalency test, once he's reached the age of twenty-one. If he passes, he can get into junior college and even some colleges. And there are plenty of high schools down south that will take northern Negro kids and help them. Nashville Christian is one. Morristown High in Tennessee is another. There are even two or three junior colleges around that will take a good basketball player and put him in a high school near the campus for a while to get him ready. In Mississippi, for instance, some leagues allow junior colleges to play high-school kids on their teams. That way a boy can play for the same JC for four or five years. I've got a boy in South Carolina at a little school who finished his high-school work in Montgomery, Alabama. He's seven feet. That helps."

Reggie Harding of the Detroit Pistons is not one of George Gaddy's big success stories, but everything finally worked out all right, with some finagling. Harding, a seven-foot-tall Negro with a typical ghetto background in Detroit, attended the Moore School for a few years until Gaddy urged him to transfer to Eastern High School. At Eastern Harding starred in basketball, but he exhausted his eligibility in his junior year. Gaddy shopped around for a place to plant Harding and made a connection with Harold Hunter, basketball coach at Tennessee Agricultural and Industrial State University in Nashville. "Hunter was going to get Reggie in," says Bob Samaras, who coached Harding at Eastern High, "but something happened and they couldn't do it without a high school diploma. So they placed him in high school at Christian Institute in Nashville, which is close by the university." Harding played one year at Christian, but by the time he was ready to enter Tennessee A&I the heat was on about trouble he had been in with the law, and he was rejected. He "laid out" a year and then signed with the Pistons as a free agent.

Gaddy did a more routine job in placing John Trapp, a Negro high-school basketball star. "Trapp was a strange case. He's a boy who flunked out of a school before he ever got into it. I had him in Ferris State in Michigan, but he just couldn't pass the tests. He went to Highland Park (Michigan) High School and graduated 148th out of a class of 148. They don't do much for the Negro kid in Highland Park. He never had a chance. I tried him around, then got him settled at Nevada Southern."

In recent years, the demand for exceptional Negro athletes has increased as various universities have decided to integrate their athletic teams. Inevitably, the recruiters and brokers beat the bushes for the superblack. Such a Negro was Al Davis, one of the most sought-after players in the history of prep football. Over 50 colleges approached him, including almost every school in the Big Ten and the Big Eight. But the University of Tennessee had a lily-white football team, and Al Davis, who had gone to school in Alcoa, Tennessee, 15 miles from the UT campus, was the obvious choice to break the line. Offered a football scholarship, Davis was taken to the campus at Knoxville and shown around, and during halftime of the Tennessee-Alabama game he was sitting on the Volunteers' bench when an assistant coach from Alabama sauntered over and said, "We sure would like to have you at Alabama but you know how things are."

Davis said, "Sure, I know."

At last the high-school senior signed a letter of intent to go to Tennessee. A message came in the mail: "Dear Nigger: go somewheres else!" But Davis had integrated his high-school football team in Alcoa and he was perfectly satisfied to integrate the Volunteers' squad. There remained the problem of passing the college entrance examinations. What happened after that is confused, and Davis will not discuss it. It *is* known that he scored high enough to qualify. But someone back in Davis' high school in Alcoa tipped off a sports writer who studied the case and wrote that someone else had taken the test for Davis. On the campus at Knoxville, it is widely believed that the student who sat in for Davis was recruited by a member of the athletic department. The university denies the report.

Whatever the truth of these charges, the Educational Testing Service, which administers the college board exams, investigated Davis' test and told him to take another examination. When he declined any further testing, the university rescinded his scholarship.

Al Davis subsequently enrolled at Tennessee A&I, alma mater of Olympic champion Ralph Boston, the championship Tigerbelles girls' track team and an all-black football team that sends more than its share of players to the pros. But the twists and turns of his abortive relationship with the University of Tennessee reveal the possibility of a corruption deeper than the ordinary white fan would dream of. As one Big Eight basketball coach says: "Things are now getting to the point where all a coach has to do is go out and pick up four or five good Negro players and let things take their natural course. In order to succeed, which means to win, he is being forced to resort to what I would bluntly call nothing else but the slave trade. What it amounts to is going out and buying colored boys who can play basketball, regardless of whether they can do any of the other things expected of college students."

"I Didn't Want to
Pick Fruit": A Study of
an Athlete Who Broke Through

5

Now and then a
black college athlete comes along who is so outstanding,
on and off the field, that he is able to exorcise his troubles
—if not all of them, at least so many that he beats the
system and becomes the personification of the word
"breakthrough." He is a *rara avis*, and he can be a
major force for racial enlightenment on the campus.
One thinks immediately of Willie McDaniel.

He emerged from obscurity about midway in the
1967 Kansas-Nebraska game, when the more perspica-
cious of the 40,000 spectators in Memorial Stadium
began to notice that a lot of tackles were being made
by a stocky Kansas defensive guard bearing the number
68. Quick looks at the program revealed only that No.
68 was Raynard McDaniel, a sophomore, 18 years old,
200 pounds, 5 feet 10 inches, a native of Florida. The defensive guard position was normally played by another
Negro, Emery Hicks, a strong 224 pounder from Nowata,
Oklahoma, who had played good ball in the opening
three games of the season.

Nebraska was rated eighth or ninth in the nation,
but by halftime the Cornhuskers had failed to score.
Fired up by a halftime talk from Coach Bob Devaney,
they came back on the field and failed to score again.
They finished the game—an upset 10-0 loser, with a
total of 72 yards gained on the ground. Afterward, when
reporters went to the Kansas locker room to find out
where the tough little Raynard McDaniel had come   **97**

from, they learned that McDaniel was a scrub who got his chance to start because Emery Hicks had been cutting classes and needed to be taught a lesson. Hicks began attending class regularly after the Nebraska game, and the two men alternated at the position for the rest of the season. They played well, and both bulked large in the Jayhawks' plan for the 1968 football season. But as the season opened Raynard McDaniel was not playing for Kansas. Indeed, it was doubtful that he would ever again don a football uniform. He turned out to be too smart—a man who equipped himself with enough of the social and cultural armor of his college to be able to tear up his athlete's articles of indenture.

Willie Raynard McDaniel's beginnings hardly suggested such an unorthodox future. He was born October 8, 1948, in the citrus town of Haines City, Florida, about 50 miles northeast of Tampa. This is a small community where the Negro population does the manual labor and the whites man the desks. The local equivalent of chopping cotton is picking and loading citrus fruit, and every year thousands of migrant workers, most of them black, flood into the area, competing for the privilege. Money is scarce; not long ago a citrus worker in the area was convicted of murdering one of his children after taking out a $2,000 life insurance policy. To escape from the life-long task of picking oranges and tangerines in 110 degrees heat and then loading 90- and 100-pound crates of fruit until their backs give out, the local men will do almost anything.

Willie McDaniel's own father, also named Willie McDaniel, toiled in the groves for 24 years, but when he got a chance to take over a ramshackle café and boarding house for itinerant workers, he jumped into the job with both feet, worked for three and four days at a time without sleep, and finally suffered a nervous breakdown. "He lost his remembrance," son Willie recalls. "He couldn't even add, he couldn't tell you what three and four was. He was in the hospital three weeks, and all he talked about was abstract things. He was in really bad shape, but he's better now. He's gained back some of the forty pounds he lost. But my mother has to stay after him all the time not to work so hard in the café. He still stays up days at a time without sleep. I don't know *why* he works so hard. I guess he doesn't want to go back to the groves."

When Willie Raynard McDaniel was living in the all-black Oakland section of Haines City, it was axiomatic among his classmates that they would wind up in the groves. "Most of my friends are still picking fruit and loading it," Willie says. "That's all they can do. Just lately they've given a few Negroes jobs as bag boys in the supermarkets, but otherwise a Negro couldn't get a job in Haines City except in the fruit business. There's not much for Negroes to do in Haines City except load watermelons from May till June, hoe orange trees, pick fruit—jobs like that. In the groves you get about a dollar and twenty-five cents an hour. If I wasn't going to college, I'd be there with the others. In the Negro society of Haines City, the high-school teachers are the upper class, and the principal is out of sight. A Negro doctor is practically unknown. Polk County has over two hundred thousand people—but no Negro lawyers, two Negro dentists and two Negro doctors. I don't know of any Negro engineers. But I know a lot of Negro fruit pickers."

Willie McDaniel is a dark, almost mahogany-colored

young man, formed in the shape of the stumpy Revolutionary War cannon barrels that one used to see in the front yards of New England town halls. You can walk up to Willie McDaniel and thump him hard across the back and Willie will bend just like those cannons. When he was a boy, he worked summers and weekends flinging heavy crates of fruit on trucks, and in his junior year at Oakland High School a teacher noticed his rippling muscles and asked him to try his hand at lifting weights. Willie pressed 240 pounds. He just thought of the barbells as orange crates. He thought of Nebraska's running backs the same way. If something weighs under 300 pounds, Willie McDaniel can handle it.

Now that he is a college man, Willie wears stark black-rimmed glasses, which combine with his large hyphen-shaped eyebrows to produce a stern professorial look about the eyes. He has small ears, a broad, Nixonesque jaw, a lumpy nose and short hair of the general texture of Brillo. When he talks, Willie worries a desk chair half to death, leaning back and forth and sideways, and although he is improving rapidly, he still tends to speak with the mouthful of mush characteristic of the Southern Negro. In conversation, Willie uses two phrases to preface his remarks. When you ask him a question, he thinks, says "you know" a few times as he considers his response, and then abruptly says, "Okay." That is the signal that he is prepared to answer the question; everything that follows will be his most serious thinking on the subject. For example, you ask him if he met any white people as a child.

"Did I meet white people in Haines City, Florida?" he says wonderingly. "Well, you know. *Hmmmmmm.* Let's see now. You know. *Ummmm. Okay!* It was an all black

100

world; I had almost no connections with the whites. The only time I saw white kids was playing once in a while. When I was about eight years old there was a place across the railroad tracks where we could do flips, and the white kids would come and watch us. We stood on top of this dirt hill and then we'd flip ourselves out into the air and land a few yards down the hill on our feet. Don't ask me why we did a crazy thing like that! I guess we were kinda showing off for the white kids. We'd always been led to believe that they were better than we were, and it was fun to show off for them. It just felt good to hear those superior white kids say, 'Ahhhhh, he can do good! Ahhhhh, look how far that one just flipped,' you know?

"After a while we started jiving around with some white kids and playing with them, but then one cat came down and said he couldn't play with me any more, and I asked him why, and we were young and all, and he said his father told him not to play with niggers. Sometimes when I think about that, I get kinda mad at myself. See, I laughed when he said that. You know? I mean, you know, I just laughed, you know? Like it's all right if he called me a nigger. He laughed, and I laughed, you know? But after you think about it some, it bothers you. I was a kid and all, but why did I laugh? You know what I mean? It wasn't that I found it amusing. Do you think I should have laughed? I mean, like *now* I wouldn't laugh. I wouldn't fight, but I wouldn't laugh. But I was eight years old. I think about that often."

A few of his friends have suggested to Willie that he stop trying to figure the memory out. They tell him that he laughed because he had to. The Negro in central Florida has very few roles: laughing, picking fruit, eating watermelon. What else was he to do but laugh? Willie has drawn no conclusions of his own. He likes to work up one side of a problem and down the other, and it is a long time before he says "okay" and announces his conclusions on the difficult problems posed by his memories of Haines City.

One day when Willie McDaniel was in his teens a remarkable event took place on a back lot of his home town. "We were talking to some white kids and I don't remember exactly how it got started, but all of a sudden we were playing football in a field; we were just playing some football together." No one could remember when white and black teenage children had played any formal games together in Haines City, and here they were in an all-out friendly contest. But it was only a short time before a police car pulled up and two patrolmen summoned the white team over. "They didn't talk to the Negroes at all," Willie remembers, "but they told the white cats not to play with us. I remember what one of them said: He said, 'It's catching!' I remember that as though it was yesterday. That football game was the only one. It never happened again."

Willie attended all-black "separate-but-equal" Haines City schools, where he feels that he learned very little. "Our teachers weren't good. You know. Look, *Okay!* You can't expect them to be very good when they went to all-Negro high schools and colleges themselves. They don't teach anything in those colleges. Have you ever heard of Edward Waters College in Jacksonville, Florida? I have a friend who's there on a football scholarship, and I was talking to him at Christmastime, and he'd been in college four months and he still didn't have a textbook, and he was passing all his courses! And this is where some of my school teachers came from.

"Personally, I know my parents were smart, naturally intelligent, but they had very little schooling. My father went to the third grade; my mother to the sixth. So it was a little deprived around the house, you know? I mean, *you* know. *Ummmm. Okay!* We didn't have books in my house. People would come around selling them, but we wouldn't buy. We had one book called the *Volume Library*, one big thick book that was supposed to be an encyclopedia—some cat had sold it to us for thirty-six dollars. I hardly ever looked at my school textbooks. From the tenth grade on, I never took a book home. My principal knew that I wasn't reading, so he tried to help me, and he started giving me books on the seventh-grade reading level, but I just read part of them and told him I'd read them all. It was boring. I'd read so slow that it bored me. I didn't even read comic books. I just looked at the pictures. Before I came to college, I had never read a book to the end."

Oakland High School in Haines City, Florida, is a typical all-black high school more or less similar to Elvin Hayes's alma mater, Eula D. Britton High School in Rayville, Louisiana, and several thousand other "separate-but-equal" facilities throughout the South. "I'll give you an idea how good Oakland High School was," Willie says, "and understand I'm not blaming anybody—it's just the system. I told you I never took a book home. But I graduated with a four-point average. Perfect! I'd go to school till noon and then I'd go to the pool hall, and I wound up with straight A's. It was too easy. We had no math in our junior and senior years. Math ended with tenth-grade-algebra; we only had one math **103** teacher in the whole school. Sometimes other teachers would try to help him out and take a course, and sometimes we had classes in the teachers' lounge, and there's no blackboard in there, so that made it tough. And half the time we didn't have any math class at all, because the math teacher was helping the principal out. Oh, man, it was something!"

High-school English, the most exasperating and most important course for Negroes, was a four-year proposition, but none of the teachers pushed it very hard. *"Okay!"* Willie says. "If they know you're gonna wind up picking fruit, why push hard on English? They offered a little French and Spanish too, and I took a semester of French, but I didn't learn anything. I got an A in chemistry, but we didn't do a single experiment the whole year. We had a lab and chemicals, but nobody knew what the chemicals were. One day a teacher showed us how sodium reacted in water. Everybody said, 'Wow!' and that was that. Once a year they'd clean out the closet where the chemicals were kept and they'd call us in and let us look at them. When I came to Kansas they wondered why I didn't know how to do experiments in the chemistry lab."

When Willie graduated from high school, he began looking around for a college. "I didn't want to pick fruit," he says. "For as long as I can remember, I wanted to go to college. I didn't know how, but I knew I was going *some* kind of way." He had been an all-star lineman at Oakland High, and now Florida A&M—alma mater of Bob Hayes and Willie Galimore and a dozen or so other superstars—was offering him a football scholarship. "But I always wanted to be a doctor," Willie says, "and the academic standards of Florida A&M aren't high enough. You couldn't get into a good medical school, coming from one of those Southern Negro colleges even if you had a four-point average." Willie wrote letters to the coaches of several white university football teams, and Jack Mitchell, Pepper Rodgers' predecessor at Kansas, offered him a grant-in-aid. Several weeks later Willie Raynard McDaniel, not-quite-typical Florida Negro, arrived on the campus at Lawrence toting all of his possessions in a single bag. Unlike most Negro scholarship athletes, he was not terrified, but neither was he fully prepared for the jump from Oakland High to KU.

"In my first two weeks here I got so far behind I thought I'd never catch up," says Willie. "I didn't study at all. Why should I study? I hadn't in high school. But when I saw the way things were going, I pulled myself together. I wanted to make A's, so I began to work."

Willie read a book from cover to cover for the first time in his life, and wrote a report on it for his first English course. The teacher told Willie it was one of the worst book reports she had ever read. "She said there was nothing right about it," Willie recalls. "Not a single word!" He worked hard on his next paper and eked out a D. On the last theme of the course, he got a B and wound up with a passing grade of C for the semester. But while he was struggling along in English he was scoring high marks in everything else. At the end of four semesters at KU, Willie McDaniel was maintaining an average of 2.6 on a scale of 3.0. After three semesters, he had nine hours of C in English, but in French he had 13 of A. In the other courses taken over the three-semester period, he had scored almost straight A's. He ranked fifth academically among all Big Eight football players, and made the dean's list in his sophomore year.

"The interesting thing about it is Willie didn't do this on sheer brainpower," says one of his teachers. "His I.Q. is around a hundred and thirty, which is high, but not all that high. The main thing he has going for him is his doggedness. If you sit down to lunch with Willie, prepare to spend the full hour. He won't be rushed, and you can't push him. He's the same with his studies. He'll stay up till two or three in the morning studying for a test, and he'll stay right on that book until he has a complete grasp of the material. Willie's no genius, but he's soundly motivated. Your genius will read a chapter once and get it, where a kid with high intelligence would maybe have to read it twice. Now Willie may have to read it three times, but the point is: he *will* read it three times."

Willie still has troubles—the typical black-and-white gulf troubles—in the classroom. "It bothers me to be called on," he says, "because I know I'm not able to express myself the way the rest are. So I try not to get called on. My vocabulary's so limited. There's a lot of things I want to say and I don't know how to say 'em, so I have to make gestures, you know? But you can't make gestures on paper. And deep down inside me I still feel inferior, you know?"

The question of Willie Raynard McDaniel's "inferiority" has been satisfactorily resolved, despite Willie's inner misgivings about himself. At the end of his sophomore year, he was besieged with offers of academic scholarships. Willie thought long and hard about his obligations to the Jayhawks' football team, the instrument of his metamorphosis from central Florida Negro to campus intellectual athlete. "Maybe I'll still play some time in the future," Willie announced, "but for this year I think I'll red-shirt [a term for a nonplaying season that preserves an athlete's eligibility] and take an academic scholarship. Then I'll have a chance to do some catching up. When I play football, all I have time for is my studies. Study till midnight night after night, only get six, seven hours sleep. But now I have a chance to catch up, learn the things I don't know. You know? *Okay!* I don't really know how to read. I can hardly socialize with college students, because I don't know what's happening. I come from another world. All I know is what I learn in class. I want to sit around and do some reading, pick up on what the white kids know. As far as I'm concerned, I don't know enough about anything."

Sitting in his little room in Pearson Hall, his legs locked in a death grip on his desk chair, Willie is surrounded by the trappings of his new life, including such books as *Capitalism and Freedom,* by Milton Friedman; *Thérèse Desqueyroux,* by François Mauriac; *Great Ideas in Psychology* (a college text), *King Lear; The Revolt of the Masses,* by Ortega y Gasset. He broke the color line at an all-white fraternity chapter, Alpha Kappa Lambda, where he was welcomed without reservation; he was planning to move into the fraternity house at the beginning of his junior year. When he graduates he hopes to attend the KU medical school, in Kansas City, and then practice medicine in some town of about 150,000 to 200,000 population—"not in the South."

"I just don't want to go back South," Willie says. "I know that a Negro doctor would be needed more in the South—that's a point—but I'd rather let my kids grow up someplace else, and then maybe I'll take 'em back to the South for a visit. I want to make it nicer for them to grow up. They'll have books around and I'll encourage them all the time. It would be too much of a handicap for them to grow up in Haines City, Florida."

Willie McDaniel realizes that he is no typical product of his deprived environment. He realizes that the white racist can torture the facts a little and prove by Willie's life (as by Elvin Hayes's) that a Southern Negro has a chance to get ahead if only he wants to. In many ways Willie McDaniel has become the symbol so hated and scorned by the black militants—the "house nigger." He realizes *that* too, as he moves to his mirror and slaps after-shave on his face and pushes a brush across his kinky hair in preparation for a dinner with the white folks over at the AKL house. "Everybody has to go his own way," Willie says, "and this is mine. The militants—I hate them and everything they stand for. I don't think Rap Brown and Stokely Carmichael believe that stuff themselves. I think they're just looking for publicity. Do they really believe we Negroes can help ourselves by shooting whites? You *know* they don't." Willie puts the finishing touches on his face, pulls on his jacket and steps into the hall to head for the fraternity house.

"We Get Sick of Going Over to Sit with the Whites": The Social Vacuum on Campus

6

Since the Renaissance, institutions of higher learning have been the scenes of social experiment. This tradition might lead a Negro to believe that if there were any place he could expect to find tolerance, it would be America's campuses. Why, then, is the black athlete held in rigid social check at so many U.S. colleges? At first glance, the answer appears cruel and oversimplified (just like some of the old ideas about Negroes): coaches—and athletic directors, who are usually former coaches—are responsible. Indeed, the coach is primarily to blame, though some responsibility lies in other areas too.

Who is this Big Daddy who strolls about the campus in spiked shoes and sweat socks and baseball cap, with whistle dangling around his neck, while Ph.D.s stand aside and point him out as a celebrity? Is he a sociologist? Seldom. Is he trained in psychology? Rarely. Where does he rank in the intellectual life of the campus? Sadly, he ranks in the *derrière-garde*. He may not be "an intellectual dinosaur," as a University of California administrator once charged of coaches in general, but he is not likely to be a Socrates or a Gladstone, either. His basic intelligence may be high or low, but so much of his cerebral energy must be applied to such matters as conditioning and play patterns and scouting and recruiting that he generally has precious little left for the human problems of his athletes. His is a more fundamental assignment: *winning*. It is also considered nice if he can carry out this assignment without rocking the boat.

These are the men who move about smelling slightly of wintergreen, barking out their orders, and guiding the college careers of black athletes—many of them deprived, frightened, maladjusted and totally unprepared individuals who come out of intellectual vacuums to make their muddled ways across the campus.

"There's all this crap about black and white," says a tough-talking and highly successful white coach. "I've told every one of my colored boys, 'You might have a black skin, but I don't consider you any different from me. When you get cut you bleed. You've got as many ribs, as many goddam teeth as me, you live and you sleep just like I do; and there ain't no damn difference, and any time you feel differently, you come to talk to me and I'll call you a goddam liar to your face!'"

One of this coach's black athletes got into financial trouble off campus, and the coach fired off a letter: "If you expect to be treated like a man and, even more important, like a human being, then you had better wake up and assume the responsibilities of a man that is married. . . . If you ever expect to enroll here on scholarship, represent this institution in intercollegiate competition, or enroll here as an ordinary student, or for that matter, enroll anywhere, then you had better have your debts cleared by registration time. . . . I am giving you a scholarship and that is more than plenty, and you still have to prove your worth. . . . Your outburst was an animal response and not becoming of a grown man. . . . Wake up and see the light and become a real man."

The same coach talks about Rap Brown: "Goddamn ignorant ---- animal!" Quickly he adds, "Not because he's black, but just because he's a goddamn ---- animal!"

110

"Animal," it develops, is this coach's favorite word for Negroes. He is known for his rages, and he can become angered at a white athlete. The difference is that the white athlete will be called a "jerk," a "dope," and "idiot." The Negro athlete will be called an "animal."

"Those are the things we notice," says a black athlete who rankles under this coach's direction. "Are they unimportant? I don't know, but we feel them just as deeply as if he walked up to us and called us niggers."

The coaching world is full of well-meaning figures who fail to come to grips with the needs and sensibilities of the black athletes who perform for them on the field. Some of the best coaches, some of the most patient and understanding, seem to have a blank space where Negroes are concerned. One of the most widely respected professional football coaches used to be head coach at a Midwestern college, and there he routinely segregated his Negro players from his white, sometimes taking great pains to order separate taxicabs, buses and dining facilities when the team was on the road. "We don't blame him for that," says one of his black alumni. "It was the tenor of the time—this was ten years ago. What did disturb me, however, was when I bumped into that same coach not long ago, and I got to talking to him about one time in Texas when we Negroes were housed 'way on the outskirts of town and had to take a long cab ride to get back and forth for squad meetings. And we also got to talking about how when we went on the road the white players were roomed together by position, so they could discuss their assignments, but the Negro players were roomed with other Negroes, regardless of position. Well, he didn't even remember the time in Texas. That tells you something. Here was something that cut deep into the memory of every black player on the team, and the coach didn't remember it at all. And he acted like he was amazed that we were hurt by being roomed together. He simply had no feeling for the problems of the Negroes. It amazed him to find we had feelings. And this is one of the nicest guys in football!"

No coach is more respected by his black players than John McKay of USC, and yet there was a time when McKay seemed to manifest this same blind spot. Mike Garrett recalls: "When practice sessions began, before school opened, the team was housed in a dormitory. We noticed that Negroes were always put in rooms with other Negroes. The same thing happened when we made the varsity and went on the road. Finally some of us went to McKay and asked him how come? He was stricken! He told us he honestly had thought that was the way we wanted it. By the time I was a junior, McKay had changed things. Negro and white players were rooming together on trips."

Coach McKay now runs far ahead of the pack. Most members of the athletic establishment will argue tenaciously that the Negro *wants* to be segregated just as much as the white man. "I remember several road trips where we'd be eating in a restaurant," says a former coach, "and I'd notice all the blacks together and all the whites together. Several times I went to the blacks and said, 'What is this, a board meeting?' One Negro asked me, 'Why don't they come to us?' and I didn't answer, but I couldn't help thinking that the whites didn't have the problem."

"We get sick of going over to sit with the whites," says a former Negro athlete, now a social worker. "It

112

doesn't do a bit of good. We go over and sit with them and right away the whole atmosphere changes. Invariably there'll be one who thinks that the way to be friendly with us is to tell the latest nigger joke. So we'll all sit down and start digging into our breakfast and this white guy'll pipe up, 'Did you hear the slogan for Brotherhood Week? *Invite a nigger to dinner!*' The whites will all laugh, to show how relaxed they are, and we choke on our Wheaties. Or you'll get another kind of white who'll have to begin a deep-think session on the problems of race. That's fine, but at the training table? Then you'll begin to hear all this forced laughter, and all these strained remarks, and pretty soon it's just too damned much trouble eating with them. Do you see my point? They are absolutely incapable of taking us as human beings. They can't talk normally to us. So why the hell should we sit with them?"

Says Harry Gunner, former end at Oregon State: "Some of the white guys don't want to associate with you because they seem to be scared to talk to you. They sort of get tense. They can't approach you like a normal guy. They can't say to themselves, 'This is another man like me.' They say to themselves, 'Jiminy, how are we supposed to treat him?' Well you're not supposed to treat him any different than you'd treat anybody else. If you got something to say, then say it!"

Dick Harp, retired basketball coach at the University of Kansas, says that the concept of sports as an integrating force is a myth in the first place, a legend nurtured by those who should know better. "Of all my Negro players," Harp says, "only one, Maurice King, ever became completely integrated. When we would go to Kansas City to play in the Big Eight Christmas tournament, King would hang around with the white players all the time. There must have been something exceptional about him, because he got along so well with the others. Once the team was in Houston, and somebody told King that he couldn't eat with the white players in the airport restaurant. He was near tears, so we all wound up eating with him in an area partitioned off for Negroes. But this was only a gesture. The rest of our Negro players spent their time off-court with other Negroes. I tried everything I could to bring our white and Negro players closer. I remember how discouraged I used to feel when my wife and I would have all the players over for dinner. Invariably, when it came time for the boys to go home, the white players would go off together in one direction and the Negroes in another.

"Sure, we broke down some of the physical segregation. We mixed white players and Negro players in rooms on the road. We did all the formal things, but the times called for more than that. What I wanted to do was reach the minds and hearts of my white players so that they would become determined not to permit the Negro to be anything less than a human being. What I had hoped was to use basketball to turn out a bunch of white college graduates who would be willing to walk that extra mile for some Negro because of the experiences they had as members of an integrated basketball team. I don't think I produced even one such white man."

Harp was Wilt Chamberlain's college coach, and he remembers Chamberlain as a sensitive loner who was close to only one member of the team. Periodically Harp would hear reports that his star center had been seen in a Kansas City nightspot, but never in the company of a teammate. "The campus at Lawrence was only a place to go to class and play basketball," Harp says. "Wilt found almost all his social relationships away from the town and away from his teammates. From the standpoint of integration, he was probably my most conspicuous failure."

Few college coaches are willing to examine themselves and their records with the brutal honesty of a Dick Harp. Most of them go about in a dream world of race, imagining that they are assisting in the slow evolutionary processes of integration (to be achieved in some century of the future, perhaps the 25th), telling the Kiwanis Club and the Rotary how much sports is doing for the Negro, and failing utterly to come to grips with the situation. And most of them have not the slightest idea what they are doing—or not doing.

What they are not doing often hurts the most, because it involves the subtlest kinds of slights. Don Shanklin recalls how he felt when he was assigned to bunk with a white teammate. "Once they brought in a real straight guy, Bob Meyers, as my roommate," Shanklin says, "and we were laying in our beds talking, getting acquainted, and I said, 'I didn't know you were white till you got here,' and he said, 'Does it make any difference?' and I said, 'Hell, no, and it never will.' He said, 'Do you know what they asked me? They asked me would it be all right if they roomed me with a Negro.'" Shanklin pauses, spreads his hands out wide in a gesture of hopelessness. "But did they ask *me*, the Negro, if it would be all right to be roomed with *him*, a white?" he says finally. "You know the answer to *that* one. But we're not supposed to notice things like that. Take our football banquet this year. The theme was Dixie. That's right. 'Way down yonder in the land of cotton.' A lot of our coaches are from the South, so they gave us all that Southern Dixie stuff and waved the Confederate flag. They sang that Southern hillbilly crap for about an hour, and there were about twenty Negro athletes there with their dates. We Negroes didn't enjoy that George Wallace stuff at all. We don't think of Dixie as some kind of emotional place that brings tears to our eyes. We know the true history of Dixie. But nobody thought of that. They had a hell of a time. Us Negroes just sat there and watched."

Shanklin is a short, heavily muscled runner who is reminiscent in many ways of the hero of Walker Percy's *The Last Gentleman.* Shanklin has been miserable and lonely in college, and one recalls a passage in Percy's book: "It was, he knew, the very time of life one is supposed to treasure most, a time of questing and roistering, the prime and pride of youth. But what a sad business it was for him, this business of being a youth at college, one of many generations inhabiting the same old buildings, joshing with the same janitors who had joshed with the class of '37. He envied the janitors."

With few exceptions, Don Shanklin and his fellow black athletes on the American campus envy the janitors. For the athletes college is a time of overwhelming loneliness, of social isolation from all but a handful of others like them. "You're reminded all the time that you're something else," Shanklin says. "If you go into the Jayhawk—that's a beer joint near the campus—you can get served, but you get the feeling you're not wanted. Most of us go to the Gaslight. They make us feel a little more welcome there. Us and the hippies. High society goes to the other places. You know what I mean by high society: white. One night a couple of white players took me into the Jayhawk and we drank some beers and jived around for a few hours, and then way down the other end of the place we heard one white boy call another white boy a nigger. See, they were having an argument and he figured that's the worst thing he could call this white boy. One of my friends wanted to go down there and fight, but I said, 'No, let's just get out of here.' "

After a while, the lonely Negro athlete finds himself pining for a single honest relationship with a white person, any white person. "Off the field you're strangers," says Warren McVea, University of Houston flanker drafted by the Cincinnati Bengals. "In my whole college career, I had one real good white friend. One time the head of the campus traffic department invited me to the birthday of his two-year-old daughter. He didn't want me to come in my uniform or my jersey; just as an ordinary person that came over and sat at his table. I was really touched by that."

If an invitation to a two-year-old girl's birthday party was one of the high points of Warren McVea's campus social life, an invitation to join an all-Jewish fraternity was one of the high points in Mike Garrett's. "All the social life at USC was centered on Fraternity Row," the Heisman Trophy winner remembers, "and this was out of bounds to Negroes. But when I became prominent because of football, a previously all-Jewish fraternity asked me to join. They wanted me to break the color line. So I joined, but I didn't stick more than a few months. I just felt out of place on Fraternity Row."

7

Al Davis, the high-
school football star who had been slated to integrate
the team at the University of Tennessee—until there
was a mix-up over his entrance exams—wound up at
Tennessee A & I, a predominantly Negro campus. He
would rather have gone to Tennessee (partly for academic reasons) but he has to admit there are some
pleasant aspects to life at A & I. "I have more time to
study here because there's less on my mind," he says can-
didly. "It's nice to be able to go across the street to the
dorm and meet your girl friend, instead of having to go
downtown—like the Negro players in the white schools."
Al Davis has put his finger on one of the biggest social
problems confronting the Negro athlete in the white university: girls, sex, "making out," a principal preoccupation of the college student and perhaps the biggest
single frustration of the Negro student.

Among the first messages passed to the matriculating
black athlete is: Stay away from white women.

The message gets across in many different ways.
Sometimes it is passed along by an *éminence grise* doing
the coach's work. When Dave Mills attended Seattle University, a Jesuit school, he had no dating problems; he
was already married. "But I knew that when a Negro
ballplayer tried to associate with white girls, he was
called in. They did everything they could to prevent
Negro players from going out with white girls. Once,
one of the fathers came to me and asked me to speak

to a Negro player who was dating a white girl. I told him I wouldn't."

Not even the great Elgin Baylor was exempt from the pressure. During his legendary college basketball career at Seattle University, Baylor elected to take a white girl to a campus ball. A coaching assistant advised him to cease and desist. "There were a few rumbles," says a school official who was there at the time, "but Elgin finally caved in."

At UCLA, generally regarded as a pleasant refuge for Negro athletes, basketball player Walt Hazzard (who signed with the Seattle Supersonics) used to feel thousands of unseen eyes when he walked about the campus with white girls. "Coach [John] Wooden never said anything to me about it," Hazzard says, "but there was always that feeling of apprehension, even when you were just going from one class to another. I remember one time, I was dating this white girl, and we were walking on campus, and we ran into an assistant football coach. He called me aside and said, 'We don't do that here.' I told him that my personal life was my own, that I was on a basketball scholarship and that he had no control over my scholarship."

Harold Busby, the sprinter and football player who anchored the Bruins' 440-relay team to a world record as a sophomore in 1967, felt the same pressure at UCLA that Hazzard had experienced three years earlier. "Sometimes if you're walking with a white girl the coaches will look at you kind of funny," Busby complains. "Nothing is said about it, but you can get the message."

Mickey Cureton, a high-school football player who was wooed by some 70 colleges before enrolling at UCLA, remembers a recruiting visit to the University **119** of Oklahoma. "Some players said, 'Don't talk to any white girl, in order to cause no conflicts, but if you do, don't tell nobody, so that the coaches don't find out.' "

Junior Coffey, star back for the Atlanta Falcons, remembers his senior year, in 1964, when he was playing first-string fullback for Washington and started dating a white girl. "That was in the middle of the season, and on the Thursday before the Oregon game I found out I wasn't starting. I went to one of the assistant coaches and asked why. He said, 'I think I ought to give you some advice. You're dating this white girl, and I'd advise you not to do it. I think it could be detrimental to your future, and it could be a reflection on the other Negro players.' " Coffey says the coach hinted that the university might stop recruiting black athletes altogether if he persisted. He remembers telling the coach, in effect, "I don't see what my private life has to do with my playing."

Junior Coffey, who was the country's third leading rusher at the time, did not start another game for the Washington Huskies. A sophomore fullback, Jeff Jordan, was moved into the position, and, according to Coffey, told him later, "Look, I know you should be starting, but don't get teed-off at me." Says Coffey: "I was mad, but I told him it had nothing to do with him. But when the guy who's starting ahead of you tells you that *you* should be playing, that's something else."

According to Luther Carr, another football alumnus of the University of Washington, "The word was never given bluntly; usually it took the form of a friendly, oblique talk with one of the assistant coaches. I remember one time one of the coaches came to me and said, '[head coach] Jim Owens loves you boys. We know you get a lot of publicity, but don't let it go to your head.' Hell, when he said 'Jim Owens loves you boys,' I just shut him off. That did it. I knew what he was talking about."

"When I went to class," says Husky alumnus Joe Jones, "sometimes I'd walk with a white girl across the campus, or have coffee with her. I never felt comfortable. I always had the fear that the coaches would hear about it. One day an assistant came to me and told me I was needed on the team and they wanted me to be happy, and they hoped I wouldn't do anything to upset the program. When that came, I knew what he was talking about—dating white girls."

Washington's Negroes tell a story about a Saturday night in 1964 when Husky sophomore fullback Claude Robert walked into a Seattle nightspot with a white date and bumped into a prominent member of the university's sporting establishment. The following Monday, says Junior Coffey, Robert found a note on his locker that said, as he recalls it: "You are no longer a member of this squad. Turn in your equipment."

"I was sore about this," Coffey says, "and I tried to get Robert to go see Jim Owens, but he wouldn't do it. 'Why should I?' he said. 'It wouldn't do any good.'"

Nor was the pressure against interracial dating confined to the football team at Washington. Bob Flowers, former U of W basketball star, says, "One time I was talking to a white girl in Moscow, Idaho, near the team bus, which was getting ready to take us to the airport to catch a plane home. It was the last game of the season. A coach came up and said, 'Get on the bus!' There was plenty of time; several of the players were still in the locker room. I got on the bus, put my bag on, then 121 came back and talked to the girl some more. We were talking about a mutual friend in Seattle. Hell, I wasn't even trying to date her—we were leaving in a few minutes. The coach got out of the car he was sitting in and came over and really chewed me out. Later when we got to Pullman, another coach said, 'We don't mind you talking to a girl, but not such an ugly girl.' Now what kind of a thing was that to say?"

One does not have to be an advocate of miscegenation to realize that such attitudes on the part of coaches force most black college athletes into a life of loneliness on the typical campus. Says Harry Edwards: "For four years black athletes live on the playing field. At a place like Utah, where they have hardly any black women, the black athletes live from season to season. After the basketball season is over, they go back to the dormitory. You see them walking around campus in their sneakers, carrying a basketball, because this is their whole life. They live for the vacations, to get back to L.A. or Chicago or Philly. When they're not thinking about vacations, they're thinking about sports. This is the only part of campus life in which they take part."

Maurice Stokes, the former pro basketball player who has been paralyzed, and in a wheelchair for 10 years (because of a game injury), has learned how to communicate through a speech therapist who can understand his painful utterances; and what does Stokes talk about? "When I got to Saint Francis College I didn't think I would last till I graduated. Life without Negro women didn't seem to be a life at all. I had to stay at Saint Francis for seven weeks after freshman initiation, without going home on the weekends. As far as I'm concerned, it was almost a living hell. They had dances at the college,

122

but I knew I would be like a thorn in a rosebush. I knew I had too much to lose by going out with a white girl."

"Nobody mentioned it, but the message got across that they didn't want you messing around with white girls," Percy Harris says of his days at Southwestern State College, in Weatherford, Oklahoma. "This was understood." To solve the problem, Harris and other Negro athletes tried to date Indian girls, "but the only Indian girls worth dating went out with white boys. They didn't fool around with the Negro boys. They always thought they were better than we were." In his junior year the frustrated Harris enrolled in a physical-education class that included social dancing. "The first time I showed up for the class I was told I didn't have to come back and that I would get a passing grade."

Student-to-student relationships are usually easier than student-coach relations for the campus Negro. The average undergraduate takes a more liberal approach to interracial relationships than the average coach—but there are exceptions. Sprinter Harold Busby remembers a national track meet in 1966, when the first three finishers in each event were to be kissed and given trophies at a victory stand. "When Charlie Greene won the hundred, Jim Hines finished second and I was third, the girl wouldn't even shake our hands." They were all Negroes. According to Busby and his fellow blacks, the girl's taste in color shadings was her own business, but who, they asked, had selected her for a role she so obviously abhorred? It was typical of the white sports establishment that the Negro's sensibilities in the matter were not considered beforehand.

On campus, the black athlete learns to accept the 123

fact that certain young women will dislike him automatically. The knowledge nevertheless can be painful to a young man in college. Darwin Campbell, a varsity basketball player at Seattle Pacific College says, "I was going to class one morning about nine-thirty, and there was this white girl walking up the steps ahead of me. She had a big load of books up to her chin, and one of them slid off. I bent over and picked it up and she turned, looked at me, and hurried off. It wasn't a look of horror or of fear, just shock, I guess, at seeing a black man. And there I was holding that book, and her hurrying off. I just took it to a classroom and left it."

Ralph Heyward graduated from Seattle University in 1965 with a degree in education, and during his college career he often crossed the color line. Now a radio account executive in Seattle, and married to a white woman, Heyward remembers his own puzzlement on the subject. "Look," he says, "you walk down the hall after a theology class, and you're with a white girl you've known a long time. Maybe in a casual gesture of affection, you put an arm around her. Here you are, coming out of a theology class, being told how everybody should practice Christianity and brotherly love—and here you are, getting cold hostile looks, all because you're seen with a white girl."

As far as white male students are concerned, the problem is merely a reflection of the old sexual attitudes that permeate society on and off the campus. Harry Gunner, former defensive end at Oregon State, explains: "The white kid thinks the Negro is better with women and girls; I mean, in bed. When he sees a Negro athlete talking to a girl on campus—the Negro is just talking, there's nothing going on—it pops into the white student's head that they have to be going to bed. It's the way he's indoctrinated. He thinks about the bad things. What he's doing, he's using us Negroes to work off his own frustrations and insecurity. What's really bothering him is *he* doesn't have that girl to talk to!"

"If a Negro guy is talking to a white girl," says Don Chaney, who went to the University of Houston, "a white teammate will come up and make some wisecrack to discourage the girl from talking to him. We had quite a bit of that on our basketball team and then the coach'd have to talk to us and bring us back together again as a team. The white athlete always automatically thinks we're doing something bad with the girls. A Negro can't be just talking. And then they'll cut the white girl socially. She becomes dirt because she talks to us, and she loses her whole crowd."

There are all sorts of variations. Don Shanklin, a running back from the University of Kansas, says, "Our football team has good squad relationships, with no apparent prejudice on either side. But if you run into one of the white players downtown with his date, he doesn't know you. It's different then. In the field house, it's 'Hello, Shank; how you doing, Shank?' But downtown with a date he turns his head."

"But when we go out with a *Negro* date," says a black athlete at Houston, "you should hear what the white athletes will say about her. They take it for granted that any Negro girl is an easy mark. They'll say, 'How was that stuff last night? That must be pretty good stuff, huh?' Imagine what would happen if we said that about their white dates! And yet *they can't see what they're doing wrong.*"

Willis Crenshaw, a running back for the St. Louis Cardinals, ruminates about an incident that happened at Kansas State University when he was an undergraduate. "A Negro was dating a white girl, and she lived with her folks right across the street from the dormitory. One of our white football players burned a cross on this girl's lawn. So since I was one of the Negro leaders in the dorm, I got the job of finding out who did it. It turned out that the guy who burned the cross was one of my best white friends! When the other white guys on the team found out who he was, they wanted to stomp him, but I said, 'Wait a minute, fellows, let's find out what's going on here.' I went to the cross-burner and I said, 'Why did you do a thing like this?'

"He said, 'Well, we saw this colored cat coming over to the girl's house night after night, and we didn't know the guy. If it had been you, it would have been different.' Can you understand his attitude? I still can't. What kind of cobwebs can a guy have in his brain to burn a cross because a *strange* Negro dates a white girl? People have all kinds of theories on why white men don't like Negroes to date their women. I don't know, man, I just don't know."

The militant Harry Edwards and his staff of bereted and beaded assistants have no answers either, but they do have some strong opinions. Not long ago an associate of Edwards was discussing the situation at the University of Texas at El Paso. "Isn't it funny that whenever you make a thorough study of the problems of white and black together it always comes out s-e-x? What a problem it must give the recruiter! They're committed to using black athletes to get their name before the public, right? So this poor recruiter has to go to the Bronx and Harlem and convince Negroes that of all the places they could go, El Paso is the best. Now, what is the first thing that enters the kid's mind—*any* kid's mind? *Are there any girls?* Well, what the hell is the poor recruiter going to say? That there are hardly any black women in El Paso and that the few single ones that do live there are usually dated months in advance? That there are only a few black girls at the university? No, he can't say that, so he has to fudge around, tell a few lies. He may even hint that the atmosphere is pretty relaxed down there in the Southwest and nobody would mind if he dated a white girl. So the kid signs his letter of intent, and then he's hooked!"

"Listen," says UTEP's Bob Wallace, who is from Phoenix, Arizona, "let me try to get one thing straight. We don't *want* to date white girls. What the hell is so great about a white girl? But we *do* want to date. *Anybody.* Black girls, purple girls, striped girls. And if there's nobody else available, then white girls. But they make it seem like a cardinal sin on this campus, *after* they've got you here."

One day a pair of recruiters were trying to convince Willie Worsley of the Bronx that he should take his wizardry with the basketball to UTEP. "We went out for a drive," Worsley remembers, "me and my father and the two guys. I wasn't too interested in what they were talking about, so I came straight to the point. I said, 'How is the social life?' One of the recruiters said, 'It's great, the sun's shining all year around.' Then they started talking about something else, but I still wasn't satisfied, so I asked 'em again, 'Well, how's the *social* life down there?' And this recruiter, he must've thought I was stupid, he said, 'Oh, it's nice, you know, the sun shines every day.' Anything that had to do with a racial prej-   **127** udice they ducked. But I was young and maybe I was stupid, because here I am. But this was my last resort. If I had had any other possibility, I wouldn't have come here."

Les Miller, a handsome young man from Nassau in the Bahamas who is part Negro, part Arawak Indian, accepted a full athletic scholarship to UTEP, and when he arrived on campus he quickly learned that despite his reddish coloring and chiseled features he was a "nigger."

"When I was a senior in high school," Miller says in his pleasant island accent, "I had a lot of offers from college track coaches. But the man from UTEP talked faster than any of the others. He told me how great this place was. He said the people were nice and there were lots of girls, and there was no racial prejudice of any kind. So I figured it must be like Nassau, where people get along together, and I accepted without even coming here to look around. So me and my roommate, Jerri Wisdom, came here and learned fast. We'd see a white girl and say hello, and she'd act like she had her ears covered, or she'd say, 'Oh Jesus,' and split. And the Negro girls—well there aren't any Negro girls. I wouldn't even know where to find them. So we talked to somebody in the athletic department about this, and he said, 'Oh, don't worry about that, boys. Just go across the border to Juárez. They practically give that stuff away over there!' That's what he thought of us. First, that all we wanted was sex, and second, that sex with those scummy two-dollar tramps from Juárez was good enough for us!"

Trackman Jerri Wisdom is also a handsome Bahamian of mixed ancestry, and he is just as bitter as his roommate. "The social life every night is, I come back to my

128

room and look at Les Miller's face. There were a few parties, yes, and there were a couple of white girls there with colored dates, but the white girls were strictly rejects. Fat, unwanted. I haven't really met any girls. Les and I have been here for eight months now, and neither one of us has had a date. I keep trying."

"I've got to hand it to him," Miller chimes in. "He don't give up. We go to class and every morning he says to this same white chick, 'Hello, my name is Jerri Wisdom,' and then he'll say it to another white chick, and another, and they just stare at him, and maybe one in a hundred will say hello back. But this guy don't give up." Someday the Bahamians will return to the islands and college will be nothing but a bad memory.

No single member of UTEP's athletic administration will admit to being dead set against interracial dating, but someone must be, because no subject has caused more trouble on the campus in recent years. According to the black athletes, there is not one coach or athletic-department member who will countenance black-and-white dating. The administration vaguely admits that this is true, though with considerable qualifying and backing and filling, and just as vaguely puts the blame on the downtown businessmen, the big contributors to the athletic program. "Some guy that's giving money to the athletic department calls the athletic director," says President Joseph Ray, "and he says, 'Okay, now I've helped for the last time. It just made me sick to my stomach to see that interracial dating going on. Now let me see you stop it!'"

Athletic director George McCarty addresses himself to the problem: "One of our biggest detriments or handicaps with the nigger athlete right now is the shortage of **129**

—you know—girls. It's their normal field just like everybody else. . . . I'll tell you what we try to do when they try to start dating white girls. It's my opinion we try to be real objective with 'em. I have set and talked with 'em before, and I'm saying that society per se in this country is really not ready for this, and that really it's not accepted on either side frankly. . . ."

Says football coach Bobby Dobbs: "Certainly, I'd say I wouldn't advise interracial dating, because I don't think it would be to the athlete's best interest as far as his future happiness is concerned. . . . No, I don't know what I'd do if I had a Negro athlete going with a white girl and he wouldn't stop. Being in this business as a football coach, I always put it this way: 'I'll tell you at the precise time it ever happens, because you don't know how you'd react under certain situations till they really happen to you.' So I don't even know."

Says basketball coach Don Haskins: "I've told my athletes that personally I couldn't care less about interracial dating, but you have people downtown who might not like it. . . . I've told the kids that I can't stop them, but I think that, well, I think that it hurts them in the eyes of the people. I've had people say something to me about it and tell me they don't like it, and I've told a couple of the kids that I think they ought to watch it, that I don't personally care, but a lot of people do."

Says track coach Wayne Vandenburg: "Sure, it's a problem, the women situation. I don't deny that. But isn't this the same everywhere in the country? This is their problem, but if a guy really wants to make it, he can find it, whether it's a white girl or a Mexican girl or whatever."

130   Though one might not want to put the statements of these men into a time capsule and present them to the people of the 25th Century as enlightened American opinion on interracial dating in 1968, one cannot fail to notice that they attempt to speak with a certain reasonableness and balance. But according to the black athletes of UTEP, the talk is hot air. They say the university's sports establishment throws out all reason and balance, where interracial dating is concerned. Pressure is applied all along the line. If the Negro refuses to shape up and confine his dating to the handful of black women in El Paso or simply stop dating entirely, he may find himself on the next train out of town. The black athletes like to cite the case of Ollie Ledbetter. As soft-spoken Willie Cager tells it:

"Ollie was a great basketball player, more promise than you'd ever want to see, and he was recruited from a junior college in Dallas. I'm not sure about his private life, but I know he had been going with this white girl for a long time and when Ollie came here she followed him and began living near the campus. We all knew about it, but at first I don't think the coaches did. We kept it quiet because we knew they didn't like things like that. Well, one night Ollie and his white girl and a couple other Negro fellows were seen getting into my car, and later on Coach Haskins called me and Willie Worsley into his office and asked whose girl she was. He asked why our group was letting itself be seen in public with a white girl, and we told him she was Ollie's girl, and then he told us to tell Ollie to keep this girl in the background, and he told Ollie the same thing in another meeting.

"It wasn't long after that we began to notice the disagreements and trouble between Ollie and the coach on the court." Shortly after that, Ollie was gone. He went on to West Texas State.

Coach Haskins, a husky Oklahoman who seems to overpower his small office, is in constant motion, like most of the UTEP coaches, and he usually looks as though he has just stepped out of a steam room. When he discusses the social lives of his black athletes, he drums the edge of the desk with his fingers and acts as though a coach who would start five Negroes in a nationally televised basketball game should not have to answer such questions. "I run Ledbetter off because he wouldn't break a sweat," he says. "He was a real good boy, but lazier than hell. Here at home where all the people are hollering, he'd give you a real good effort, but on the road he wouldn't break a sweat. And I was afraid that this would become contagious. Ollie had more ability than any man you've ever seen. Matter of fact I helped get him into West Texas, and I almost went down there and got him off the bus, I felt so bad about it. Yes, it was known that he had a white girl friend, but I couldn't do anything about that when I knew about others doing the same thing. Some of them are smarter than others about it."

Haskins may insist that Ledbetter's social life had nothing to do with his departure, but there is hardly a Negro on the campus who will agree. Says Dave Lattin: "One day Coach Haskins called me in and told me that somebody had said I was holding hands with a Mexican girl downstairs in the SUB [Student Union Building]. I told him, 'Well, listen, if I was gonna hold hands with somebody I would do it right out in the open.' And he said, 'Well, you know that you and I would fall out if you did something like that.' Right then we were something like eighteen and 0 for the season, and he's all hot and bothered about me holding hands with a Mexican girl! So I said, 'Well, I hope we don't fall out, but I feel like I should be able to do what I want to do, as long as I'm not breaking any laws.' But after that I cooled it a little."

Bob Wallace, who was a second-round draft choice of the Chicago Bears, got the message in his sophomore year at UTEP. "There was a white girl helping me with my studies and we got pretty tight," he says. "Some sorority called Coach Dobbs and Coach Dobbs told me that the people wasn't ready for this yet. He said if it was up to him, I could do whatever I wanted to, but he said if I kept on seeing this girl, him or I would have to leave, and he would prefer it to be me. He said he was aware that there weren't very many Negro girls in town and he said, 'I know you guys have to do something, but when you finish playing ball for me you can do anything you want in this town, I mean I wouldn't care.' But if I kept going with the girl, I would have to go."

Wallace did not stop seeing the girl, but he says, "I had to be careful. I couldn't take her into the center of El Paso. I had to take her across the border on our dates or maybe to a drive-in, something like that. I just had to kinda keep it quiet, you know?"

"The coaches always tell you the same thing: that the town's not ready for it," says Fred Carr, who was recruited by the Green Bay Packers. "But I think it's the other way around: I think the town is ready for it, but the coaches aren't. I think the tail is wagging the dog. What the hell, I come from Phoenix, Arizona, and nobody thought nothing of dating white girls over there.

Phoenix isn't that far from El Paso, and the people aren't that different. But our coaches are mostly Southern types, and interracial dating is a big scandal to them. And you don't only get that from the coaches. Some of the professors and a lot of the students will tell you the same thing. They think they're being helpful, and if you don't take their advice and you get yourself seen with a white girl, you get in trouble and she gets bad-mouthed all over the campus."

"I used to talk to a white girl," Willie Cager says, "but one day she said to me that she couldn't talk to me any more because some of the professors had been telling her that she would get a bad name."

"If we show up at a party, the white girls have to leave," says Bob Wallace. "If they stay they'll get bad-mouthed. One time we showed up at a party and there was a white girl there and she stayed. One of the white football players went back on the campus and called her all kinds of dirty names."

"That's another reason the white girls hate to date us," says runner Les Miller of the Bahamas. "She's gonna be finished on the campus."

Says Dr. John West, head of the English department: "I have a grader who cares a lot about these Negro athletes. She grades in this huge class of a hundred and thirty, and she takes the roll for me. She says that people do look oddly at her, and I have heard a comment or two to the effect that 'I think old Sonya has fallen in love with the Negro race' or something like this. And then the blond girl who tutors them at night, she says she's gotten some stray looks that are pretty ugly when she just walks across the campus with one of them. But I don't think we have any professors who would

134

give a girl a bad mark because she was dating Negroes. I don't think that it goes that far."

According to at least one attractive coed, Professor West is wrong. She is blond and she is beautiful and she dated Phil Harris, who was a legend on the UTEP campus, a sort of black Paul Bunyan, towering six feet ten inches into the dry, desert air on feet so big that "It requires the hide of two steers and a yearling to shoe him," according to the 1966-1967 UTEP basketball yearbook. As the yearbook also advised, "Harris holds a lot of 'ifs' for the Miners. If he can improve his shooting; if he can take up a lot of slack inside and if his defense improves, the Miners could come on stronger than frozen cement this fall." The Miners did not come on stronger than frozen cement. They compiled a soso 14-9 record. As the yearbook said of Harris before the season began, "He is the only experienced big man Coach Don Haskins can summon." And he was not there when Haskins needed him. Pressured to stop dating his blonde and later placed on probation, he was finally expelled.

Why was such a potentially valuable athlete as Phil Harris dropped? The record is vague, and no UTEP official cares to come up with a precise answer. There was a matter of parking tickets, which Harris claims he did not start getting until he began dating a blond; there was a report for dormitory-rule violations; an ashtray he may or may not have thrown and a remark he may or may not have made in an El Paso store.

George McCarty tries to explain how Harris came afoul of the administration, but he is hard pressed. "I don't know *how* to explain it. Phil never did anything bad. He was continually doing the marginal. He would disturb a class, or he'd go by the swimming pool and they'd maybe be having a class and he'd talk real loud and the teacher'd ask him to be quiet and he'd just ignore her—that type of thing, not real bad. But marginal, you know? He had more chances than anybody here. More than the law allows."

Presumably, the rights and wrongs of all this are buried in the files of the disciplinary hearing held in Harris' case. But one thing he definitely did do was get engaged to his green-eyed Caucasian beauty and show her off proudly around the campus.

"It wasn't that Phil didn't know his place," says a white teammate. "He knew it, but he defied it."

Harris' refusal to follow the wishes of the UTEP establishment may have had nothing to do with his expulsion. UTEP officials repeatedly say that it did not. All that is clear is that Harris, already on campus probation, became involved in an argument with a dormitory manager on a Saturday, and an ashtray was broken—Harris says he accidentally knocked it off a table. On Monday morning, he was told there would be a hearing on his case that afternoon, and a few hours later, having ignored the warnings he says he got from coaches and from George McCarty that his pro basketball career would be affected and that he would be asked to leave school if he didn't stop seeing his girl, he was through at UTEP.

During this period his fiancée was having her own troubles. "For a while, nobody knew we were dating because we didn't dare let anyone know, the way things were," the girl says. "We used to go over to a friend's house and watch television for a date, things like that. But word got out, and one night the landlord of my dormitory called me in and asked if I thought I was doing the right thing. He asked if I thought my parents would approve. I said I was almost twenty-one. He said, 'Don't you think you could get something better?' I told him there *wasn't* anybody better.

"When school opened, Phil and I knew we loved each other and we were going to get married, and that's when we decided we shouldn't have to sneak around anymore. So we went to a football game with some of the other basketball players and their dates: four white basketball players, four white dates, me and Phil. When we walked in, thirty thousand pairs of eyes stared at us. The phones were ringing all over the campus that night.

"Then a good friend came to me and said she couldn't be my friend any more. She said her fiancé had told her that she couldn't be seen with me now. One night a dorm counselor, a woman, just stood there and screamed that I was a nigger lover. Phil would call the dorm and leave a message and I'd never get it. Sometimes he'd call and say who he was and the girl would hang up. So he had to get one of his white teammates to call, but they wouldn't give me those messages either."

Harris' girl, a member of a well-to-do Eastern family, had been maintaining a good average in a complex course of study.

"About the third week of school," she says, "I was at a social event by myself and one of my professors was there. Somebody warned him that he'd better not talk to me socially because my boyfriend was six feet ten. Well, that gave it all away, because Phil was the only person that tall on the campus. The professor approached another friend of mine and he said, 'Do you mean to

137

tell me that she dates Phil Harris?' Then he started talking about how he disapproved of interracial marriage or interracial *anything*. Later he told somebody else that a girl who dated a Negro would get nothing but an F from him. Well, that's the way it was. At the end of the marking period, I had one C and all the rest A's and B's, except for the F.

"I was so upset I looked at somebody else's tests and lab reports, and my work compared well. This other person got a B. I got a low mark in my finals and I'd done especially poorly in my essay questions. Well, it's hard to argue about essay questions but I took my paper and textbook to the teacher and I showed him where one of my 'wrong' answers was almost an exact paraphrase of the text. He told me that was too bad; that he disagreed with the text. I took the whole case to the head of the department, and he told me, 'You got what you deserved.' "

When it was all over, a member of the faculty athletic committee said he would be happy to sum up the case of Phil Harris, provided that his name not be mentioned. "White guys get it tougher than Phil Harris got it," he said. "People tend to over-react to these racial matters. We leaned over backward to be fair and not to be racist in the Phil Harris case. The white girl complicates things, obviously, *but not in our minds*. Not in ours, not really, but in other people's."

"I Didn't Know What a Birthday Cake Was": A Look at Life on the Black Side

8

That whites and Negroes live in two separate worlds is a bland axiom for whites and a grim fact of life for Negroes. The troubles of the Negro athlete in a white world stem largely from the failure of whites to examine the axiom; their unconscious assumption is often that the black athlete on entering the white world leaves his own. But the facts of life never yield so easily, and the divisions between the worlds remain. They are deeper than most whites can imagine, for they involve wholly different attitudes toward even such basic matters as food, money and responsibility.

To white athletes food is something that is ladled out three or more times a day, consumed and largely forgotten. To Negroes, food is a fascination, a preoccupation, an obsession. "Our colored athletes will spend their last dime on food," says Bobby Dobbs, white football coach of the University of Texas at El Paso. "They are a people that can go and eat in a chow hall, but if they've got any money later that night, they will be over at the Wiener schnitzel or the fried-chicken place. I don't think the white race puts that premium on food. It's more important to a Negro. Some people say that's because Negro children go hungry a lot. But I just think it's inherent with their race. That's what they live for, is to eat, I think."

One is always meeting members of the sporting establishment who feel that certain characteristics of the average Negro are "inherent with their race." Tags and nickel slogans are popular in the world of sports, and the Negro athlete spends his life in a tight mesh woven of the white man's prejudices, clichés and sweeping simplifications. Only rarely does anyone in sports stop to puzzle the problems out, to approach Negro problems as social problems, and then more often than not he will be a Negro himself, like Melvin Rogers.

"They say we like to eat," says Coach Rogers, "and I say I agree; brother, we love to eat. And you take any white American who was brought up poor in the depression years and you'll find somebody else who loves to eat, and that's how simple the problem is. The depression never ended for the Negro; hunger is something he lives with, and he's gonna shovel that food down any chance he gets. Two years after he becomes financially stable, he's still shoveling that food down, trying to fill that hole in his stomach. Ten years later he's not much different. Inherent in the race? Not any more inherent than poverty."

The boys who go out for Coach Rogers' baseball and basketball teams at Eula D. Britton High School in Rayville, Louisiana sometimes make him shake his head sadly as he stands in front of them trying to make the first cuts from his squads. "There are about two hundred boys in the high school, and from those two hundred you lose about fifty right away: polio victims, mental or physical defectives, a few with rheumatic hearts, some with asthma. Out of the remaining hundred and fifty, you find maybe fifteen or twenty who are good enough to play ball. The rest of them just can't make it. Diet is one of the main reasons."

One year Coach Rogers put a six-foot-tall boy into a

rigorous training program to strengthen him for basketball. The program called for long-distance running, starting with the mile and working up to the five-mile run. The boy ran and ran, but he was never able to get past the two-mile barrier, and it almost broke him in half physically to run that far. One morning Coach Rogers visited the boy's home in Rayville's Blacktown. "They were having beans for breakfast. The mother was cooking bread, and she explained that the bread she cooked in the morning was for the whole rest of the day. I asked her what else they had besides bread, and she said, 'Oh, mostly just bread. And sometimes a little greens.' Well, it was too late for me to do anything about that boy in high school. But look what happened. He's four years out of high school, twenty-two, twenty-three years old, and he's just now reaching his full growth. He's playing for a neighborhood basketball team, and he's plenty good. And he'd have been all that big and all that good in high school, if he had been eating something besides bread and beans."

One year the teachers at Eula D. Britton made an informal survey and found that the average student was coming to school without breakfast. "So we started a program serving juice in the morning, and next year we're going to try to serve more than that," Coach Rogers says. "But you run into certain problems. Some of these kids have almost never had milk; they can't afford it. Now they get milk automatically with the twenty-cent school lunch, and they won't drink it. They haven't had a chance to develop a taste for it. They wind up passing it along the line to the next kid. So I tell my athletes to get in line behind those kids that don't drink milk. Somebody's got to drink it; might as well be my athletes!"

Indeed, the technique of hustling extra food at lunch-time has become a fine art with Negro high-school athletes, most of whom come from the same deprived homes as the other Negro students and yet require more than a normal amount of sustenance. Rogers is not the only coach who instructs his athletes in special techniques for getting extra milk. At Don Chaney's high school in Baton Rouge, the athletes were advised to get in good with certain girls who had not developed a taste for milk and others who refused to eat beans in public because they felt it was socially degrading. "Some days I would have six or seven cartons of milk," the lanky Chaney recalls. "I'd even carry a few back to class with me. And beans! I could get all the beans I could eat."

At Don Shanklin's all-black high school in Amarillo, the athletes learned how to make sweet eyes at the cafeteria assistants in order to win bigger helpings. Willie Cager of the UTEP basketball team used to take a quarter in lunch money to school in the Bronx and try to run it up to 50 cents in the crap game that always went on in the hall. "Usually I made it," he says. His teammate Willie Worsley cultivated the Jewish students at De Witt Clinton High School in the Bronx. "Jewish fellows don't eat too much at school," Worsley explains. "They get so much to eat at home they're just bored by the cafeteria food. So there was always plenty of meat and stuff left over, and I got plenty."

But not every Negro athlete is so lucky, or so clever. Some achieve years of athletic success on diets that would not sustain Tiny Tim. Bill Myles can show you dozens of them. Myles is a Negro who played center for Drake University's football team and returned to the black world as football coach at all-Negro Lincoln High School in Kansas City, Missouri. "Sometimes I go to coaching clinics and hear some white coach tell me all the problems he has with the white fathers—they complain that their sons are being discriminated against or that some other man's son is getting bigger write-ups in the paper. How can I talk to those coaches about common problems? My problem isn't how to deal with an irritated father, but to go out and buy a box of Cream of Wheat and half a dozen eggs, so that one of my players and his family can eat for another day. As for newspaper write-ups, most of my kids and their parents never even read a newspaper."

Myles laughed. "Last winter, the basketball coach at Southwest High School told me about one of his boys coming up to him and saying, 'Coach, you're lucky to have me at practice today. I almost went to Paris with my father for the weekend.' Imagine a father doing that for a son! When I want to reward my kids I tell them that if they win I'll take them to McDonald's for hamburgers. Or I may tell a boy, 'You score a touchdown and I'll buy you a barbecue dinner.' But *Paris!* What do you think of that?"

During 1967 Myles began to realize that he had a potential professional athlete on his hands, a boy who could run the 60-yard dash in 6.2 seconds and the 100 in 9.7, and who rushed for 960 yards and 13 touchdowns in his senior year; the boy had half a dozen colleges panting after him. One day Myles went to his address and found that he was living in a friend's car and scrounging for food on the streets. Myles got the boy a job at the school so he could afford an occasional warm meal. As soon as the boy began eating, he began doing better **143** work in the classroom. "He'd been spending too much of his time figuring out how to eat," Myles says. The boy's name is Robert Buford.

The night before he was interviewed, Robert Buford got caught in the rain, and while he was running home he tripped and fell in the gutter. In the house he began to ache all over, so he changed clothes and went back out in the rain to go from door to door looking for aspirin. After a fitful night's sleep he cadged a glass of orange juice and went to his classes at Lincoln High. He had no money for lunch. In the afternoon, Coach Bill Myles tucked Buford into a cot and under two blankets. He lay shaking and quivering through the interview—a very black boy, slightly built (five feet ten, 163 pounds), with a Floyd Patterson haircut (close on the sides and full at the front), a large nose spread over the middle of his face, completely unmatching miniature ears and quick smile that revealed an uneven line of white teeth. He said it was a long story, how he wound up living in a car:

"When I was young I was shipped to my grandparents' and my aunt's a lot. I never did be around my father and mother very much. Everything was pretty nice when I was small till my mother and father separated, and then they started taking me here and there. At that time it was only me and my brother and my sister. My brother's in Omaha now and my sister's in Chicago and I'm here in Kansas City. From six years old on I have been shipped around. I stayed with my mother for about three years and then I came back to my father and stayed with him till I got thirteen years old, then he went to Denver, so I stayed with my other auntie. Then I went to Denver with my father. Then I came back. Then I went to Great Falls, Montana, to stay with my mother for a while. She wanted me to stay for good but I didn't want to. She was having another . . . another baby. I told her I wanted to come back to Kansas City, so she brought me back.

"Then I lived with my grandfather and grandmother. I stayed with them until my grandmother died. Then all of a sudden my grandfather started putting me out of the

144

house and all like that. Then I went back to my auntie and then after that, I went to my cousins, after me and my auntie had a misunderstood. Then I came back. Then my auntie just split and I began to stay by myself. I spent the nights with my friends for a while, and then I started staying in cars. I didn't want to go to Omaha and live with my father because Omaha is not fun, like it is down here in Kansas City. It's real bad in Omaha because my brother is always getting into so much trouble. And if I go up there I would be in the same thing. Down here my friends will talk you out of it—and tell you to keep going on.

"I stayed in different cars every night till the beginning of last football season, when it started to get cold. I only had the clothes I was wearing. The only time I could take a shower was when my body started to odor and when I went into a friend's house they would smell me (that would be embarrassing), and they would tell their son to have me take a bath at their house. Sometimes I felt ashamed 'cause I hate to come to anybody's house like that. And then I would go right back out in them cars again. Now that I have twenty-three dollars a week coming in from a job at school, I live in a one-room apartment with a stove and a icebox, a bed, a chest and a table.

"For Christmas, my uncle got a Ban-Lon shirt for a gift and he passed it on to me. My grandfather gave me five dollars, and he said he was going to give me something else for Christmas, but I haven't got it yet. My father didn't give me nothing for Christmas. When I realized my father wasn't giving me nothing, it made me feel kind of bad. So I went on and tried to forget about it and do the best that I can, just as though he had gave me something.

"The people in my family were surprised that I kept on going to school after they put me out of the house. They thought I was going to do like my brother and quit school and hang out in the streets like they said I'd been wanting to do for a long time. Ever since I was small, when I first went out for sports, my people has always been throwing things and hitting me and beating me, saying that I'm lying that I stayed out late because of practice, that I was just hanging out in the street. When I tried to tell them, they never listened. So when I got good in sports, then they kind of brag on me, and that is what I hate. Now that I am doing something, they say, 'This is our boy, he did this and he did that.' They always say that. So the only people I ever ask to help me is the coaches.

"Every year we have a dad's banquet for the football players, and there never is many dads that show up. But last year my father came up from Omaha and I felt real proud because the year before I didn't have nobody to come up. The last time that I saw my mother was five years ago. Sometimes I have hatred for her and the man she's living with. He beats her all the time, and then I feel sorry for her. So far I know she's got seven kids.

"When I start having kids, I ain't gonna do them like I see most parents. I'm gonna help them out when they're small, and when they get a little older I'm gonna still help them. Like I need my father's help and he's never around. I'm gonna be around. My father had a habit of always beating on me till I started fighting back. I might whip my own kids, but I won't go half-crazy when I do it. I always gonna keep my kids close and feed them and always think about them.

"I been in trouble, yes, but not a whole lot. I have only been in jail once. When I was young I was arrested two or three times for riding stolen bicycles. And then I was caught in an old house getting copper and stuff to make money. The big time was when my brother went to Kansas and stole a car. I was driving it and got caught. They put me in jail for a day even when I told them I didn't know the car was stolen. Back before I wanted to be a professional football player, I always wanted to be a hustler. Every time you would look up, the hustler would always have money and was always driving these big cars. Then I met this man who worked in construction and had money and a big car too, so then I said I wanted to be in construction. Everything I saw I wanted to be. That was before I started playing football. Then I wanted to be a professional football player, and I still do.

"When I'm gonna play in a game or run in a track meet, I try to always get lunch. I have to bum money—ask people to give me a nickel or a dime—and most of the time I don't eat. I never eat breakfast, and sometimes I miss the lunch meal and the evening meal too. I used to starve a lot. But I would keep on trying. Before games I'd always go around and try and get something to eat. I was always sick, but I never showed it. I would try not to run lazy so they wouldn't know nothing was wrong.

"This year the coach got me a job, helping out around the school, and then when I set a new meet record at an indoor track meet the school nurse baked me a birthday cake with my name on top of it. I didn't know what a birthday cake was, and it wasn't my birthday anyway, so she told me to pretend it was. We cut my cake at school and it lasted about five minutes, but it was good. School's not really such a bad place. I wake up at six o'clock and get to work at seven. I clean out the gym and then I talk to the fellows. My first class is metals and it starts at eight-fifteen. We're working on the vise now. We made our screwdrivers and our tool trays. After that I go to English class and I don't like it. I got three right out of one hundred on my English test. Most of the time I don't read. I don't write much either. After English I go to woodwork and after that I go to lunch. Then after lunch I have choir and then woodwork again and then gym. I don't go to gym that much. They do a lot of baby stuff, and most of the time I skip sixth and seventh periods and go play pool. The biggest thing I learned in high school was how to run with a football. I learned a little in class too; I used to get a thrill cutting open frogs."

Talking to Buford (he does not like to be called Robert or Bob, just "Buford"), one begins to get a chilled feeling. All through his recital of misery and despair, he sounds neither miserable nor desperate. And suddenly one realizes that Buford is merely describing life as it is. He knows no other. Moving from a grandmother's place to a cousin's place to parked cars to a friend's house to a one-room apartment is *normal;* never eating breakfast is *normal;* barely knowing how to read is *normal.* There is not a hint of self-pity about Buford, nor does he compare himself to other, luckier boys. He knows no luckier boys. In Buford's lexicon, a bad boy 147 is one who goes to the penitentiary for a long term. A hungry boy is one who has not touched food in two or three days. These are everyday definitions in the Negro ghetto of Kansas City.

Buford will not graduate from Lincoln High School—he will receive a certificate of completion that says merely that he was a good citizen and endured his allotted time in the halls of learning. He is a special student and goes to special classes. According to Coach Myles, Buford's mentality is average: "He just can't read." But he has heard about college, and he is desperate to go, not only for social reasons but as a stepping stone to pro football. "The only people who put the college idea into his head were the college coaches," says a Lincoln teacher, with the air of a man who sniffs disaster. But Buford is exhilarated by the idea; he thinks he will go to junior college to catch up and then accept the best scholarship offer.

Ten years ago, Robert Buford would have breezed right out of the Kansas City ghetto and into any one of dozens of colleges that wooed him. Nowadays standards have been tightened, and it will not be so easy for him to attend college. But attend he will. Robert Buford represents too great a temptation to certain American schools that are selling themselves to the public on the basis of their athletic reputations. Some institution somewhere will yield to the temptation he offers, and Robert Buford, with his woodworking credits and his slow reading speed and his near inability to write, is more than likely to wind up on a tree-lined campus, posing as Joe College.

Buford represents an extreme, but by no means can he be considered atypical. Every year hundreds of Robert Bufords find themselves on the campus, drowning in a sea of problems: money, where to get it, how to handle it; schedules, how to meet them; temptations, how to avoid them; classes and homework and meetings and chalk talks, and practice, practice, practice. Do most of them learn how to solve the problems? No. The gulf is too wide. Most Negro athletes remain on the black side forever.

Coaches go through agonies trying to shepherd their black athletes across this gulf, and seldom succeed, and for their troubles they usually have only themselves to blame. Coaches are paid to win, not to solve social problems, and if a Negro with straight Ds in electric shop can run the 100 in 9.4, there is always a coach willing to recruit him. And when the trouble starts, it is the fault of the Negro, "inherent in the race," never the school. Listen to a typical coach:

"I recruited him myself, drove two thousand miles to get him. Fixed it up so he could go to a high school in town to bring his grades up. So he comes here and all of a sudden he's married, and he hasn't got a penny to his name. So I lend him money. I move the boy and his wife into my own apartment. My wife and I are feeding them, cooking their meals; they're living with us. Finally we go out and get them an apartment, and I pay their deposit. The athletic director calls me in and he says, 'Cut that out! You're gonna get fired if you keep it up!' But I pay the kid's first month's rent and buy him a month's supply of groceries. The next thing I know, his wife's pregnant, and we get him fixed up with the doctor, no bills, no nothing. And after all this, we find out two things: the kid isn't gonna pass his courses, and the way things are going in his private life, he isn't going to help us on the playing field, either. Now is that ungrateful or not?"

One morning this particular athlete woke up to find himself in a strange town, married, 19, a father, living in a tiny apartment, and stripped of his athletic scholarship. At college he had been an independent operator for the first time in his life, and he had failed. How could it have been otherwise? His previous life in the ghetto had taught him only that money was something you won in a crap game or slipped from a woman's purse, and responsibility was something that happened on the other side of town. Who was to blame for his situation? The coach will swear he was blameless, and pull out the IOUs to prove his point.

In every college that recruits Negroes, financial problems are commonplace. To the average Negro, perched way across there on the other side of the gulf, money is another country. He knows as much about handling cash as the average white student knows about handling Norwegian rats; they are equally rare in their cultures. "Here's a kid that came to this university without a dime," says a track coach about a black world-class athlete. "Now he has a 1966 car. His apartment is out of this world. He spends thirty or forty dollars every chance he gets. He's got the very best of clothes. He's got two television sets. One for the bedroom and one for the living room. Big ones. Consoles! He bought a five-hundred-and-fifty-dollar RCA stereo, the best money can buy. I slip the kid money whenever I can. I made him money on the indoor circuit. I'm not supposed to, but I did. He wants everything, but he hates to pay the price. So he's up to his ears in debt." The athlete is handling money for the first time. He is like a looter standing in

front of a broken pawnshop window. His needs are greater than his sense of responsibility. For the poor, it
comes with the territory.

"Negroes are prone not to accept their responsibility
and this is because of their heritage," says a Southwestern university athletic director. "It'll come with
education. Say they've got a telephone, they make long-
distance calls. They're indiscriminate about it, they don't
realize you've got to pay, and they're prone to get over
their heads, and then they think, 'Well, I don't really
have to pay this today or tomorrow. . . .' I fault the business people. These kids'll go into a store and get credit.
They buy things and they don't seem to realize they
have to pay, and this aggravates us."

Negro athletes are constantly aggravating their coaches, and few coaches take the time to dig down very far
and find out why. It is simpler to announce that a lack
of responsibility is "inherent in the race," like a love of
fried chicken or a predilection for candied yams and sow-
belly. A Midwestern coach whips out a list of athletes
who are behind on their laundry bills. There are seven
names, all of them Negroes. "Do you get the message?"
he says.

Another Midwestern coach discusses the subject: "I
would say in all honesty that ninety-nine percent of the
disciplinary problems on this team are caused by Negroes. Things like being late to class or study hall,
delinquencies in small debts, failing to do the required
work, things like that. And the last guy to turn out for
practice, just at the last second, is usually a Negro. It's
almost as if they're testing you to see how far they can
go. Most of them simply have not been educated in responsibility. They aren't so much in rebellion against   **151**

authority as they are just plain irresponsible."

Another coach bristles with anger when he discusses the Negroes on his team; one wonders why he recruits Negroes at all, but then one remembers that this coach is a winner, a *nationally known* winner, and it is the Negroes who have been winning for him. He seems to approach them as a necessary evil. "They drive me crazy, off the record," he says. "I wake up at night screaming. Little things. The Chinese water torture. Not long ago one of our Nigra athletes looked like he was gonna flunk right out of school. He wasn't passing anything. And we sorely needed this boy on the team; I mean he was *crucial*. So we sat down and discussed the problem and came up with a solution. We would get him tutors, and the athletic department would foot the bill. I mean private tutors; every college kid's dream. never showed up! Night after night the tutor'd be there and the boy wouldn't show. And then the Nigras go around telling how they never get an opportunity!"

"Well, about this problem of irresponsibility," says Don Chaney, "up until very lately the Negro knew he was gonna be chopping cotton or running around hauling the white man's trash, or something like that, and he knew he wasn't gonna go to college and he knew he wasn't gonna get a good job and he knew he wasn't gonna get out of the slum he was raised in. *Well, he doesn't have much to look forward to, does he?* So they call him lazy and irresponsible. But there's one little thing a human being has to have, and that little thing is hope: H-O-P-E. If you take all hope away from him, he's gonna say, 'Well, why should I jump up and hustle and almost kill myself when I'm not gonna get anyplace anyway?' Then you hear white people saying that the Negro isn't punctual. Well, if you're gonna spend you life chopping cotton, it doesn't make much difference if you're punctual or not, does it? That cotton's still gonna be there waiting for you, isn't it? That sun still be shining whether you're five minutes late or ten minutes early, am I right?"

Harry Edwards, the militant Negro professor from San Jose State College, says, "You talk about accepting responsibility. Well, I say to you, you take a newborn black child and you put him in a big black box with a closed black top and you open up that top when he's twenty-one, and you say, 'Now, boy, you go do my work!' Is that a fair thing to expect him to measure up to a white child who you never put in a closed box?"

"We Make One Mistake
and We're on the Bench": Playing
the White Man's Games

9

Almost any college coach will tell you that the second the opening whistle blows and the game starts, all prejudice goes out the window. The white tackle who has been telling "nigger" jokes all week smashes a black halfback to the ground and then graciously helps him to his feet. Prejudiced attitudes are discarded and lineups are fashioned from the best men for the job, regardless of color. The black forward who has been hanging around the white girls' dorms all week starts the game anyway, because this is America and we play to win, and no matter what differences we may have off the playing field we pull together without regard to race when it comes to the day of the game.

The scene is pleasant, but it bears no more relationship to reality than some of the old ideas about the characteristic odor of the Negro race and the thickness of their skulls. There is every bit as much racial prejudice after the opening whistle blows as before: it comes from coaches, trainers, white players and fans.

Coming from the coaches, the bias is not always apparent, because everything a coach does in a game is reckoned as a personal choice aimed at bringing home the victory, and can always be justified as such. "Sure, I took Johnson out in the second half and put in the white kid. I didn't think Johnson was doing the job out there today. Yeah, I know he made eight tackles in the first half, but he had a lot of help on them and I'm the coach and I make the decisions and I'm the one who gets hell if we lose and it didn't seem to me that Johnson was cutting it. Race? Are you kidding? I'd start a purple-striped baboon if I thought he could help us!" The logic is so pure that it is seldom scrutinized.

Can the mythical Johnson go to the NAACP and lodge a complaint of prejudice? He can, but he is likely to be laughed out of the office. Americans of all colors find it hard to believe that a coach would risk losing a game just to work off some of his racial prejudice. Coaches find it hard to believe. But they do it all the time, not only on the college teams but also in the pro leagues.

Harry Gunner, former defensive end at Oregon State, remembers a game against USC and its star O. J. Simpson. "I had just come back from an injury," Gunner says, "and nobody knows better than I do that I wasn't at my best. But I still was out there trying to do the job. Now O. J. gets the ball and he runs around the other end, and the defensive end, a white boy, doesn't force quickly enough and O. J. almost goes for a touchdown. That's okay; everybody makes mistakes. But now comes the second half and the same play, but this time around my end. I make the same mistake as the white boy and O. J. picks up five yards. I look up and a substitute's coming in. I spent the rest of that game on the bench. Everybody on our team was whooping and hollering and enjoying the game, but I couldn't whoop and holler and enjoy it."

Negro athletes are almost unanimous on one point: They have to be better than their white teammates. "A white kid can make five or six mistakes and stay in," says Don Chaney, an alumnus of the University of Houston basketball team. "We make one and we're on the bench." And if a black player and a white player have equal ability, the white player is much more likely to start. The Negro athlete has to be what Muhammad Ali once called himself: "Superspade."

Even if he is superbly talented, the Negro athlete may come to grief against a quota system. On the University of Kansas football team, the Negro players are convinced that there is a very formal quota system and that it is rigidly enforced. They say Kansas will never play more than two Negroes in the backfield, and seldom more than three on the whole offensive team, and only a few more than that on defense. "What they do," says Don Shanklin, "is they take the skilled Negroes and stack them at one or two positions and let them fight it out, while the white players get their positions automatically. The reason is simple. The fans don't want to see too many black faces on the field at a time. The heroes are supposed to be whites. That's why they allow a few more Negroes on the defensive team. Not so many heroes are produced there."

When it comes to stacking black players in certain positions and operating rigid quotas, Kansas (which has been going through a period of agonizing reappraisal about its black athletes) may even be one of the lesser offenders. At the University of Washington, stacking and quotas have been almost a tradition. Says alumnus Junior Coffey: "In 1961, Jim Stiger played fullback for Washington and led the team in rushing. The next year they moved him to right half, with another Negro, Martin Wyatt, behind him. This meant that there would be only two black starters in the backfield, the halfbacks. I was a sophomore, and I was put behind Bobby Monroe, a white, at fullback; Monroe did most of the starting, but I eventually gained most of the yardage."

Negroes at Washington say that stacking began as long ago as 1956 and has continued ever since. They point out that in 1958 there were five Negroes stacked at left half—Luther Carr, George Fleming, Carver Gayton, Tony Softlie and Bernell Anderson. "You see," says Carr, "we Negroes can only run to our right!"

The next year, 1959, it was Fleming and Gayton at left half, Ray Jackson and Joe Jones at fullback, all Negroes. In 1960 it was Fleming, Gayton and Charlie Mitchell at left half, Jackson and Jones at fullback. Negro alumni charge that the arithmetic was simple: only two Negroes could start in the backfield at a time. There have been adjustments since then, but the quota and the stacking continue.

According to Sandy Green and some of his black teammates on Tommy Prothro's UCLA team, stacking goes on there too. "During my junior year," the defensive back says, "I started the first six games and then they yanked me and put a state senator's son in my place. They had to play this guy someplace so they tried him at one of the positions where there were Negroes."

This, of course, is only Green's view. Other Negroes on the UCLA squad, with future eligibility that Green did not possess, refused to discuss the matter for the record. They claimed that a coach called them in after an article about Negro athletes appeared in LIFE and told them that they would be cut if they talked to the press about racial matters. The coach denied the charge. When a black reporter called on him, he opened the interview by handing over a printed statement: "I certainly realize that nationally and in most communities there is a racial problem. However, if we ever had **157** a problem, we certainly do not now. Our squad unity is most gratifying."

Most of the Negro players disagree. They say there was frequent racial dissension in 1967 ("That's why we lost the USC game," says one. "Because we weren't really a team"), and that there is a firm double standard up and down the line; the athletic department, they assert, keeps a tight rein on black athletes and lets the whites run loose; Negroes are stacked into certain positions; the school helps white players get housing and jobs but does little for the blacks; white players exclude the blacks from many of their social events, and blacks are pressured to stay away from white girls. One keeps reminding oneself that these Negro athletes are talking about UCLA, nationally known as a "paradise" for black athletes, the school that has thrice elected Negroes to the presidency of the student body, the school that numbers among its alumni Rafer Johnson, Arthur Ashe and many another famous Negro athlete.

The essential white attitude about the Negro on the playing field is not simply the standard American attitude that the Negro is inferior, stupid and immoral, one step up from an orangutan. The essential attitude is that these are white men's games, as indeed they are. All the Negroes playing football for American colleges back when Paul Robeson was starring for Rutgers in 1917-1918 would not have filled the "colored only" waiting room at the railroad station in Waycross, Georgia. Until a decade or two ago, Negroes who wanted to play pro basketball had to learn to clown like animals before they had a chance to try out for a single team: the Harlem Globetrotters. And even today, two decades **158** after Jackie Robinson integrated "the national game,"

Negroes on college baseball teams are distinguished by their almost total absence. At Michigan State, for example, Negro football players have won the school national fame, but in the past 15 years there have been only three Negroes on the varsity baseball team.

These are white men's pursuits. The Negro may integrate them, or even almost take them over, as in college and pro basketball, but the essential character of the game, the ethics and folkways, remain white—and basically Anglo-Saxon. (The Negro player is the successor of all the men with Irish and Scandinavian and Central European names who have given so much to games developed by men with such names as Walter Camp of Yale and Percy Haughton of Harvard.) The Negro may be permitted to help out, but his role is clearly defined: he is a hired performer, and he has a job only so long as he knows his place in the white game and stays in it. Says Warren McVea, former University of Houston flanker: "Whatever happens to you out on that field, you know the white players are thinking two things about you: that you're some kind of superhuman because you're black, and that you're dumb."

"One time I couldn't get a play," says Don Chaney. "I kept making the same mistake over and over, and the guys were kidding around and laughing. But I knew deep down what they were saying: that I was a Negro, therefore I was dumb. And you sometimes hear them make cracks about the football players. They'll say, 'He's dumb, he can't remember plays, he's got to line up with a notepad strapped to his wrist.' And you notice it's always the Negro players they're talking about."

During the 1967 season Warren McVea was involved in a blown play that resulted in the Houston quarterback being smeared. A white teammate, Ken Hebert of Pampa, Texas rushed McVea and began shoving and berating him, and McVea shoved back. After the brief set-to, Houston fans began to ride McVea. He had stepped out of his place. He had acted human. Presumably he should have let Hebert knock him down, apologized for his stupidity and begged forgiveness. Because he did not, he is still known in parts of Houston as the "smart nigger" who had the effrontery to stand up to a white man in front of 41,000 people.

The white character of college football is amply displayed at the University of Washington, where the athletic department has worked for years establishing a mystique called the "Husky Way." According to the black players, the "Husky Way" is simply a euphemism for the "White Way." "What is the Husky Way?" says Gregg Alex, repeating a bitter stock line among the Negro players. "A Husky is a man from a third-string high-school squad who can run the hundred yards in eleven seconds, who is a robot, and you make an All-America out of him." Says football player and trackman Dave DuPree: "There are a lot of white 'Huskies,' but I don't know of a single black 'Husky.'"

The difference between the white or "Husky" way and the black or "soul" way shows up most clearly before a game. For as long as sports historians can remember, the white way to prepare for a game has been to sit around and look somber, serious, almost funereal. Too much is at stake out there tonight for any joking around. Anybody who cracks a smile is not taking this ball game seriously enough. "Black athletes look on it as a game," says a Washington football player. "We're relaxed. But the coaches will look at you and frown, if you're not getting yourself all psyched up for the game like the white athletes do."

The same problem arose in 1968 with UCLA's national champion basketball team, built around Lew Alcindor and counting heavily on two other Negro starters, Lucius Allen and Mike Warren. Without its Negroes, the UCLA basketball team would have been nothing, and everybody on the campus, including the Negroes, knew it. Thus some breakthroughs were forced in the white character of the game. "We three black players knew that as a unit we had a lot of power," says cocky Mike Warren, "and we did a lot of things that would not have been tolerated otherwise. Before the season Coach Wooden told Alcindor and me that our hair had grown a little too long last year [they were wearing it in bushy "naturals"] and suggested that we cut it closer this year. We didn't, and nothing happened. We also changed the pregame routine. Most Negroes don't get ready for games, like white people. We don't have to psych ourselves up. Before we got on the varsity, the locker room used to be quiet before a game; everybody was supposed to be concentrating on the opponent. But now we just sit around and talk 'til it's time to go out on the floor. When the white players saw us talking, they started talking too, and everybody was relaxed."

But not every team has a reasonable coach like John Wooden, and not every team is built around three black stars like Alcindor, Warren and Allen. On most teams the Negro is expected to take abuse—and keep his mouth shut about it. Sometimes the abuse comes from his fellow teammates and the opponents, but more often it comes from the coaches.

University of Kansas football players watched with

amazement during the 1967 season as a peculiar relationship grew between a Negro player and a white assistant coach. "It started when the player made a mistake in practice and the coach kicked him kind of half seriously and half playfully," remembers Willie McDaniel. "When this happened again, the Negro just laughed—he's that kind of kid, he takes and takes. So now the kid would be down in a crouch ready to do a forward roll in practice, and the coach would come up behind him and kick him! And then laugh! And then all the white cats on the team would laugh too. It got to be the big joke on the team, and this kid weighs two hundred and thirty pounds, and he's getting kicked every time he goes into a crouch. I'll tell you one thing: it wouldn't have been the team joke if the coach had been kicking me!"

A double standard exists. It can be understood in terms of certain racial remarks that lose their steam, lose their inner appeal for the sadistic and masochistic impulses of whites if some other word is substituted for "Negro" and its cognates. Would anyone have laughed if a comedian had said, "There's an Anglo-Saxon in the wood pile?" How much attention would have been paid to a book called *Little White Sambo*? Would the University of Kansas football team roar with laughter if its white quarterback Bobby Douglass were kicked in the tail repeatedly by an assistant coach?

The double standard also involves injury. As every white racist tells himself, "The nigger likes to dog it." This attitude—that the Negro is lazy, and he feigns injury—pervades the sporting establishment.

In any discussion of such matters as a double standard of injuries—in fact, in much of the black-white controversy—it is important to remember that the Negro is reacting from the viewpoint of the insulted party. If he cites 1,000 examples of a certain prejudice, the point is not the weight that can be attached to the individual examples, because sometimes they sound petty or childish, but that the condition as a whole does exist, and that it *is* a grievance to the black athlete. Says Willie McDaniel of KU: "Thermus Butler, one of our Negroes, had a hurt shoulder, but he still had to run and work out in practice. But one of the white players had a cold and he was excused. One day I had a sprained ankle, and when I came out on the field wearing a gold jersey, which is the sign you're hurt and don't have to practice, one of the coaches made me run all day, around and around that field till my ankle felt like it was gonna break right open."

Negro athletes tell many stories about the treatment they get from white trainers (complaints about trainers arise repeatedly among black athletes who have voiced their problems to college administrations) on those occasions when the coach is willing to admit that there is indeed a *bona fide* injury. Dave DuPree swears that a trainer at the University of Washington sent him out to play football with torn tendons in both hands. After the season, he was hospitalized for surgery.

Walt Hazzard says he knew a UCLA football player who injured his wrist in an early game and was told by the training staff that he had nothing but a sprain. "He played all season with his wrist taped up," says Hazzard, "and after the last game they told him he'd had a broken bone in his hand. He wound up in a cast for eighteen months." Hazzard claims he himself had a hairline fracture of a bone in his right leg but was not told about it until the end of the season. "It came out in **163** the training room," he says. "A player made a slip of the tongue. The point is, they just don't think a black athlete can be hurt. The black athletes have a little private joke about that. When somebody's hurt, the saying is 'Okay, spit on it, rub a little dirt on it; you're fine!'"

The case of Warren McVea sums up the injury situation, and what is meaningful is not McVea's attitude but that of a Houston athletic department member. Mc-Vea's grievance is a general one covering his whole college career: "If we say we're hurt, they say we're faking. I played four years with injuries. I played my whole senior year with a pulled groin muscle; it made it hard for me to cut and change speeds, and that's my game, twisting and spinning around out there. Before every game they'd shoot me full of novocaine and send me out. It wouldn't have been so bad if anybody had known about it; it's only human to feel better if people know you're hurt and you're still doing your best. But the coach told me to keep quiet about it. He wanted me to go through the whole season playing crappy games without telling anybody about it."

"Mac is no complainer, and he's telling you the truth," says the member of the Houston athletic department. "He was hurt almost all the time he was here, and yet you hardly heard a word about it. People didn't *want* to hear about it. Somehow they couldn't accept the idea that a Negro athlete could be hurt."

The black athletes, to use Walt Hazzard's phrase, have to "rub a little dirt" on their mental injuries as well. The University of Washington training staff kept a bulletin board in the training room, and the board was adorned with pictures of players on a scrub team 164 who had performed outstandingly well. For a while, one Negro, Al Roberts, was represented, but his photograph was missing. Instead, there was a cartoon of an African native, complete with a bone through the nose. When Negro team members scratched up the cartoon, some of the trainers were angered. They acted as though it was not the Negroes' place to take such a step.

The word "nigger," with all its painful connotations for the black athlete, is used as a psychological weapon on the field. Corky Bell of the Loyola of Chicago basketball team remembers a time during the 1967 season when the opponents used the word repeatedly. Loyola frequently started five Negroes: "The standard joke was that we were starting four niggers and one albino," Bell says. "I'm the albino, because I'm light-skinned." In the game that Bell remembers best, the use of derogatory names like "nigger" was so frequent that he became suspicious. Later one of the other team's substitutes said that his coach ordered the players to use the word "nigger." The coach had hoped it would get the Loyola team upset.

Sometimes the mental pressure comes from teammates. Percy Harris, a coach at Du Sable High School in Chicago, remembers competing for a tackle position with a white athlete in college. "We were practicing this one-on-one blocking and after you block you're supposed to tail off and go around and wait your turn, but this guy said, 'Let's go again.' So I block him again and he says, 'Let's go again.' This goes on about five more times. On the sixth time I says to myself I guess I'll put an end to this, so I pushed him twenty or thirty yards down the field and when I stopped blocking him he starts swinging at me, and by that time the coach was there and broke it up. That boy was an All-America, but there was something about having to compete with a Negro that bothered him."

The fans have plenty of ways of expressing their own prejudice. When Darryl Hill worked out before a football game at the University of Maryland, he would notice that cheers would go up from the crowd when he dropped a pass or a kick, and boos when he caught the ball. Once, the whole Maryland football squad left Clemson stadium dressed in football gear, fearing trouble from the crowd because of Hill's presence on the team, and again, in South Carolina a drunken fan tried to spill his drink on the young Negro as the team left the field. "The player behind me noticed and bashed the guy with his helmet," Hill recalls.

In Hill's judgment, the toughest place to play was Virginia. "Those students were mean," he says. "They gave our Jewish linebacker, Jerry Fishman, a bad time too. They'd yell, 'Get that dirty Jew off the field!' They were the most vocal by far." Hill also got his share of threatening phone calls. ("You come into the stadium and we're going to shoot you," one caller promised.)

Such calls were not restricted to Virginia, nor is the display of racial prejudice during games exclusive to the South. When Darwin Campbell was playing basketball at Seattle Pacific College the team journeyed to Yakima for a game with a junior-college team. Yakima is a conservative fruit-growing and farming area in the eastern part of the state, and the local John Birch Society chapter has a firm foothold in the town. The game had hardly started before Campbell began to hear the shouts. "A bunch of fellows had seated themselves down close to the sidelines right in the middle of the court. They took up about the first three rows.

166

Every time I'd get the ball out of bounds, I'd hear them say something like, 'Tuck in your shirt, black boy, you're getting enough notice.' I got real mad about it, but I didn't let them get to me. I scored eighteen points that night, and we won."

Lee Evans, the record-holding San Jose State College runner, thought he had left the red-necks behind when he went to Innsbruck, Austria, with a group of American trackmen, in 1966. But Evans was going through his hotel lobby when he passed a group of Southerners, one of whom said loudly: "Those damned niggers! I don't care *where* we go. We can't get away from them." The next afternoon, Evans, by then the toast of Innsbruck walked into the lobby bearing his trophies, and the same Americans tried to shake his hand.

When Dick Harp was coaching basketball at the University of Kansas, he heard certain sounds from the cheering sections whenever he started a few Negroes. "They'd play *Sweet Georgia Brown*, the Harlem Globetrotters' theme song, when our boys came on the court, or they'd take the Kansas yell—'Rock Chalk, Jayhawk, KU' —and change it to 'Rock Chalk, Blackhawk, KU.'"

Lately the pressure on the basketball team has relaxed a little at KU, and the starting line-up occasionally lists four Negroes. But Harp made the breakthrough. He began to think of quitting his job as Kansas coach on the day he found himself wondering whether it would offend the Kansas spectators if he started four Negroes. "All four of them deserved to start," he says, "but the mere fact that I had to think about it brought me up short." Harp played the four and kept on playing them, but he grew tired of the insults from the fans and the digs from the alumni, and in 1964 he resigned.

10

Shortly before the St. Louis Cardinals' Bob Gibson took the mound in a 1968 game to try to equal Don Drysdale's record of six consecutive shutouts, he was asked if the pressure of the situation bothered him. "I face more pressure every day just being a Negro," he said.

"You know those junk yards along the highways in Jersey?" said Larry Doby, former Cleveland Indian and the first Negro ever to play in the American League, and now an insurance salesman in Saddle Brook, New Jersey. "Well, they have scrap heaps just like that for athletes—most of them black. Black athletes are cattle. They're raised, fed, sold and killed. . . . Baseball moved me toward the front of the bus, and it let me ride there as long as I could run. And then it told me to get off at the back door."

"Man, put that pen away," said Curt Flood of the Cardinals when a Negro reporter began to ask him about race relations. "The next thing you know I'll be playing in Tulsa."

Gibson was bitingly serious, Doby deeply bitter and Flood only half kidding. Though all three are baseball players and the remarks of each were directed at a different aspect of the problem, all were answering the question of whether the professional Negro athlete is viewed as an equal—more or less. The pro sports establishment would maintain that it is a bastion of racial equality. But in spite of 20 years of progress, the professional entrepreneurs still prefer their Negroes in the back of the bus.

To be sure, the life of the average black pro athlete is much better than that of his counterpart on the college campus. The professional faces few of the problems that are causing so much unrest among black college athletes. The professional can have a measure of dignity and a degree of financial security. He lives in big cities where his social life can be normal and where he can find limited acceptance. Above all, he does not have to contend with a scholastic regimen and an intellectual community that he is totally unequipped to face.

But he does have racial problems, significant ones, some of which are markedly different from the college athlete's. He watches helplessly as bigotry and discrimination on and off the field erode his earning power, restrict his opportunities for success and deny him part of the reward for his achievements. He must be measurably better than a white man playing the same position. He must accept the stacking of Negroes at certain positions in order to keep other spots open for whites. He must face up to quota systems—only so many blacks per backfield or per infield or per team. He must cope with instances of personal prejudice (teammate racism, though diminishing, has severely hampered numerous teams in various sports).

These are aspects of its operation that pro sport would like to keep quiet, but the Negro professional is no longer going along with the gag. Like his collegiate counterpart, he is talking. Negroes have had so much to gripe about that, listening, one sometimes feels the gripes will survive the justification for them. But grievances, whether based on fact, on imagination or on a mixture of both, are still grievances. The Negroes' list of them is chilling, and they must be acknowledged.

Nor is the problem any longer restricted to a handful of players. The degree to which Negroes have moved into pro sport is astonishing. More than half the players in the National Basketball Association are Negroes—as were eight of the 10 starters in the last NBA All-Star Game. A quarter of the players in the National Football League are Negroes, and the 1967 All-NFL team was 40 per cent black. Nearly 25 per cent of all players in major league baseball are American Negroes, and here too a disproportionate number of the stars are not white. For example, of the top 10 hitters in the National League for the 1967 season, only one was a Caucasian.

But in spite of this imposing success, the black athlete still finds that he is playing a white man's game, and the white man is not only running the show from the front office, but applying his old stereotyped concepts to the task.

In baseball, the Negro usually will find himself in the outfield, less often playing in the infield, and least often performing as a member of the battery. Only 13 of the 207 pitchers in 1968 major league rosters were Negroes. In the pro football leagues, those streamlined models of modern professional sports perfection, the Negro is never permitted to be a quarterback. The black college quarterback wants that pro contract as much as the next man—perhaps even more, because there are far fewer ways for a Negro to make big money. But he knows that he has no chance to play his position in the pro leagues. So what does he do? He switches. He *anticipates* the white man's categorization of him, and acts accordingly.

In his native Long Beach, California, Gene Washington was not only a prep passing star but student-body president of an integrated school. At Stanford he played quarterback on the freshman team, and in his sophomore year he beat out veteran Dave Lewis for the starting quarterback's job. In his junior year, 1967, Washington suddenly emerged as a flankerback. The impression on the campus was that another player had beaten him out, but the truth was that he had initiated the change himself. "It was strictly a matter of economics," says Washington. "I knew a black quarterback would have little chance in pro ball unless he was absolutely superb. What usually happens is that the pro team tells you there's no place for you at quarterback, but they can use you as a defensive back or flanker. And then they tell you they can't give you as much money because you'd be learning a new position. So I decided to beat them to it. Now when I deal with the pros, I will deal for the most money available to me at my position."

Rigid pigeonholing of black athletes occurs throughout pro football. Though most people realize that there have been no Negro quarterbacks, few stop to think about other positions. On one typical weekend in the 1967 NFL season, *no* Negro center started a game. Of the 32 offensive guards in the starting lineups of NFL teams, 29 were white. That tight little interior cluster of men—center, two offensive guards and quarterback—was as lily-white as the Alabama state police. "It's not very complicated to figure out," says a white NFL player. "The play *starts* right there in that cluster. The center has to get the ball off on exactly the right count and then cover his man. The two offensive guards have to know how to stand fast and block to one side or the other and they have to know how to pull the hell out of there and lead the play around an end, and they have to know how to head fake and shoulder fake and everything else, because the other team is watching them and the center to try to figure out where the play's going. Those three guys and the quarterback are *it*. It doesn't make a damn what the other seven players do; if anybody in that tight little cluster screws up, that's it. The play is dead. Now how can white coaches, with all their built-in prejudices about the Negro, assign positions like that to black men?"

Race also distorts the situation at linebacker (on that same typical weekend in the 1967 season, 48 linebackers lumbered out on the field to start NFL games, and 45 of them, or 94 per cent, were white): "Most defensive football players have a single job to do, with little variation, but the linebacker has to exercise judgment," says a thoughtful NFL player. "He may wind up tackling the quarterback fifteen yards behind the line of scrimmage, and he may wind up knocking down a pass twenty yards up the field. He has to be able to read plays —well, everybody knows all the things the linebacker has to do. It's one of the most responsible defensive positions. Therefore, he can't be a Negro. The exceptions are guys like Dave Robinson who are so good that no coach would have the guts to play him someplace else. In other words, a few Negroes can break through these white preconceptions, but only if they're superplayers, and believe me, Dave Robinson is."

To the white management the perfect position for the black athlete in pro football is cornerback. The position requires speed, a commodity that most Negroes bring to the game. And it requires very little of that quality that the white man likes to think belongs exclusively to him: judgment. "Cornerback is not a brains position," says Bill Koman, retired St. Louis Cardinal linebacker. "You pick up the split end or the flanker and you stay with him all the way. That's it."

On that same typical 1967 weekend in the NFL, the picture at cornerback was a crowded scene of black faces. Three fourths of the starting cornerbacks (24 out of 32) were black. In fact, the ratio of black to white cornerbacks was almost exactly the reverse of the ratio of black to white players of all types in the league.

"Yassuh, white man, boss," says one NFL cornerback derisively when asked about this situation. "We ain't got the brains to play center, 'cause we can't count, but we can follow that flanker's ass all the way down the field, *yuck, yuck.*"

The average Negro high-school player tries to program himself into the glamorous offensive positions, and it is from the ranks of these high-school backs that pro cornerbacks are made later. There are few pro teams that care to start three Negro offensive backs; the customary maximum is two. Though the coaches deny it, of course, color becomes a factor when they assess their player needs at draft- and tradetime. A team with a black fullback and flanker will take a very good black running back but would still prefer a white one, and will draft accordingly. Talent remains the most important criterion, but color *matters.*

As a result, those young Negroes who insist on playing certain positions in school and college—instead of changing their positions to fit the white man's idea of what they should play—often have problems when they go to the pros. "You find yourself getting switched and

173

doing everything backward," says Bobby Mitchell, Washington Redskin flankerback who was an All-Big Ten halfback at the University of Illinois. "Then you start getting extra coaching and you tense up because now you're thinking about every step. The next you know, you're fouling up all over, and then bang! You're cut! But I've seen white football players who were switched from their college positions and started messing up and they were sent back to their old position to regain their confidence."

"There are a lot of variables in this problem," says one NFL player. "Remember, the idea in pro football is to create white heroes to please the white crowd. Negroes play cornerback, because cornerback isn't what you would call a heroic position."

Buddy Young, the Negro All-America from Illinois who now works as Commissioner Pete Rozelle's assistant in the executive suite of the NFL, takes a different position. "The black must learn that he is not a pick-and-shovel athlete, that he is capable of playing anywhere, that there are no restrictions but those he creates or accepts," says Young. Young seems to be suggesting that stacked positioning is something the Negro player himself "creates" by not fighting against it from high school on. But he ignores the fact that, except for the Negro superstar, a black athlete who fights the system does so at the risk of his career.

The lamentable truth is that professional football is as infested with prejudice and discrimination as the college game. But the student who tries to pin down the exact locus of the discrimination in pro football—or in other pro sports—finds himself at a loss. Man for man, 174 most members of the professional football establishment will tell you that they grapple Negroes to their souls with hoops of steel. "Why, the Negroes have made this game what it is today," says an AFL administrator. "Why, we'd have had a hell of a time without them!"

That's not the way the players—including some white players—see it. Says one white member of a Century Division team: "The prejudice takes really strange and subtle forms in the NFL. I can say in complete honesty that I can never remember a coach mentioning a guy's race or color. I can't cite a single case of a player who was cut because he was black. I can't remember a single Negro-white fistfight except one or two that had nothing to do with race. But the prejudice is there. The league reeks with it. The way the teams are composed. The way Negroes are criticized more than whites. The way they're not supposed to know how to play certain positions. The way the white players are allowed to boss them around and criticize them. But if you accuse anybody of being prejudiced, you get a lot of fancy rationalizations and explanations: how this coach fought to keep a certain Negro on the team, and therefore *he* can't be prejudiced, and how that coach makes regular trips into Blacktown to recruit Negro stars, so *he* can't be prejudiced. All those things that make them sound like big liberals. If I were a Negro, I'd go nuts trying to fight it, because you can't fight it. Where do you start? It's like attacking a wall of mushroom soup."

In examining race prejudice in the NFL, for example, one encounters such research material as the fact that 11 of the 15 starting NFL quarterbacks in 1966 were from the South or the Southwest, either by birth or by college affiliation. That statistic looks meaningless, until one talks to a Negro end who wonders whether he gets passed to as often as he should. Who knows? Pro football authorities will say the very idea of such a form of prejudice is preposterous, and any pro quarterback will say it is absurd to think that the color of his receiver matters—that he discriminates. Statistics can't be compiled on matters like that.

Similarly, no one keeps records on quotas, and there is no way to tell what the black quota is on each team, without reading the owner's mind or attending front-office conferences. But quotas are a routine fact of life in all professional sports.

Though owners and coaches shudder at the thought of being held responsible, they are the ones who establish the quotas. In maintaining quotas, the management of a team thinks it is giving the fans (i.e., the whites) what they want. Psychologically the fans have to be able to identify with the team, and how can white fans identify with black players? But fans also like a winner, so the general manager must work from two curving lines on the graph of his club's success. One charts performance, the other identification. The more star Negroes he uses, the more performance he is likely to get. But, he reasons, the more Negroes he uses, the less white fan identification he gets. It is where the two lines cross that a quota is established, one that varies from city to city, sport to sport and team to team. Nothing is more obvious in professional sport than the fact that there are quotas—and few facts are more hotly denied.

"There are quotas on every NFL team and always have been," says Bobby Mitchell of the Washington Redskins. "Paul Brown was a pioneer in the extensive use of Negroes, but eight or nine was about it. The Redskins had about seventeen to twenty most of last year. That was high, and I bet we won't be that high this year. Do you really believe that when a coach says, 'I'll take the best player at the position,' he means it?"

One hears all sorts of rationalizations for quotas. "Negroes are moody," says Chris Burford, former Kansas City Chiefs' pass catcher. "They tend to range higher and lower emotionally than white players. If you get in a game on a day when a majority of them are moody, then you can be in trouble if you are playing a lot of them. To me, seven to ten is the ideal number of Negroes to have on a football team."

There are not many pro coaches who operate on the premise that Negroes are moody and therefore ought to be held to a minimum, but many coaches do hold to the viewpoint that individual Negroes can have the wrong "attitude" and cause team trouble. "The white man is always interested in your 'attitude,'" says Jim Parker, former All-League tackle for the Baltimore Colts. "You have to have the right 'attitude' or you can't play. At Ohio State I had a friend who I thought could play a good game, but the coach said he didn't have the right 'attitude,' so he sat on the bench for four years. Even in pro football you look at a guy and you think he can play, and then one day he's on the train going home; something to do with his 'attitude.' You worry about it, but you don't ask any questions because you have a family to feed."

Pro coaches will go out of their way to avoid drafting a Negro with the "wrong attitude," and there is evidence that such blackballing is practiced throughout both the NFL and the AFL. Robert Lawrence "Bobby" Smith, six feet three inches tall and extremely fast at 190   **177** pounds, was a starting defensive back at the University of California for three years, averaging 290 minutes of playing time per season. When he played in the East-West game and the Hula Bowl, the pro scouts seemed very interested in him. "After the regular season I was told that I would be drafted," Smith says, "possibly as high as the second or third round. I was told this in person by one scout, and I also heard it from those who said they were speaking for three or four clubs."

Then the Cal campus erupted in a dispute between black athletes and white administration. The Negroes had complained that a black basketball player was told he would be benched if he did not cut his hair, which he was wearing in the long "natural" style favored by militant blacks; they also claimed that the off-campus housing available to them was substandard. The protest led to the departure of the head basketball coach. The spokesman for the black militants turned out to be Robert Lawrence Smith. "I used to be a good nigger," he explains, "but now I was one of the bad guys."

The pro draft took place a week after the disturbance, and Bobby Smith was ignored. He was not so much as invited to try out on any team in the NFL or AFL as a free agent, which is the least that happens to any superior college football player. Smith is bitter. "If they can draft jailbirds [Cincinnati had drafted an imprisoned Michigan State defensive back], why couldn't they draft me? I'll tell you why: because they go by the creed to 'keep them grateful.' I guess I wouldn't be grateful enough."

In pro sports, an "ungrateful" black might indeed find enough inequities to keep his team in constant turmoil. Segregation is still more or less the norm; blacks stick with blacks in the dining rooms and whites with whites, and the periodic campaigns by white players to blend the two colors never achieve any lasting results, partially because it is so hard for a white to overcome the Negroes' distrust.

Sometimes the segregration is imposed by the team itself, and the athlete either takes it or speaks out and risks losing his job. Clemon Daniels, star running back of the Oakland Raiders, is one who speaks out. "I play for a pro club, and there should be no segregation problems. But you wonder. Out comes the rooming list on the road and all the blacks are paired, except on this club where we had eleven blacks, so one was given a single room."

Says Al Attles of the San Francisco Warriors: "One time I was looking over the hotel list and I noticed check marks behind the names of all the black players. I asked, 'What's the reason for those marks?' The man said he didn't know and took away the list. It's a subtle thing. You know, but you don't know."

Mike Garrett sometimes finds himself wondering about the Kansas City Chiefs' front office. "Since so many of our boys are from the South, I can't help asking myself the question: Is that why when we go on the road Negroes are always roomed with other Negroes?"

Until recently, a sort of unspoken agreement between black and white consigned the tallest and huskiest white players to the front or first-class section of the Chiefs' charter plane and all the blacks to the back or economy section. "Originally the idea was that the biggest of the white players needed lots of space to be comfortable," says Garrett, "so they grabbed those big first-class seats. It was a kind of continuation of the back-of-the-bus idea." But there were big Negro players too, and stocky   **179**

muscular ones who wanted to relax in comfort on the
flight home. Finally Bobby Bell, a Negro linebacker,
walked to the front section and deposited his six-foot-
four-inch frame into one of the first-class seats. The
other Negroes watched from the rear to see what would
happen. The white players murmured a bit, but did nothing. "I told myself, 'I want to sit up there too,' " says
Garrett. "So I did." And that was the end of the Kansas City Chiefs' segregated airplane.

The average fan has no idea of the everyday pressures
and tensions that exist between Negroes and whites on
almost every professional team. Pro athletes tend to be
prima donnas in the first place, supermeticulous spe-
cialists who push themselves to the limit and punish
themselves unreasonably if they fail. The players can
be just as harsh on one another, and sometimes the play-
er-to-player tensions can become violent. A white player
on one AFL team called a black player a "dirty nigger"
and was soundly beaten up for his remark. But such
scenes are far more rare now than they were a few
years ago. Mike Garrett likes to point out that his own relationships with white players are excellent. He particularly mentions E. J. Holub, a Chiefs' linebacker from
Texas. "The great thing about Holub is he keeps after
you to do your best whether you're white or Negro, and
if you don't, he rides you equally hard. That's all I ask.
I want to be taken for granted, not coddled or patronized
or loved or hated because of my color."

Beyond such paramount matters as quota systems
and man-to-man prejudice, the black professional athlete
makes two other major complaints: that he must be sig-
nificantly better than his white counterpart while he is
active, and that when he is through as a competitor,

his sport has no use for him. It is in baseball that these two aspects of the black athlete's career show themselves most clearly.

In terms of the militant postures of today's young Negro society, baseball is almost an anachronism. The biggest single move of the black team athlete into the consciousness of America came when Jackie Robinson was brought up to Brooklyn in 1947, and it is argued by some that baseball has been resting on its liberal laurels since. Conservative by nature and hell-bent to maintain its profit curve, baseball has kept rigid control over its athletes—black and white alike. At a time when black athletes are being put under heavy pressure to pour energy and prestige back into the Negro community, it is rare that a black baseball player is heard from. Curt Flood was kidding about being sent down to Tulsa, but the specter of the minor leagues is too real for the average baseball player to risk offending the front office.

"Baseball players can't stick their noses out and say things about racial injustice like a Russell or Chamberlain," says an established major league star. "We can't negotiate for ourselves because of the reserve clause [which, in effect, makes the player the exclusive property of his club during his baseball career]. There are no other leagues. Either you sign with your team or you don't play baseball."

It is rare, therefore, for a Negro baseball player to talk about the disparity between what is expected of him and what is expected of the white player, but the difference exists, and the Negroes are well aware of it. "We have to produce a lot more, to stay around," says a major leaguer who was typically insistent about not being identified. "There are plenty of white guys who've been around here fifteen years with lifetime batting averages of .240, but you don't see many Negroes around like that. And you don't see many Negroes sitting on the benches, either."

A statistical study by Aaron Rosenblatt in the sociological journal *Trans-Action* documented with shocking clarity how much better the Negro has to be. It showed that in the seasons of 1962 through 1965 the average American Negro major leaguer hit 21.2 percentage points better than the average white major leaguer. (Pitchers' batting averages were not included.) Approximately the same percentage pertained to the previous nine years. The conclusion was obvious, and Rosenblatt drew it: "More places are available in the majors for the substar white player than for the comparably able Negro."

But of even more importance to the Negro is the fact that when he stops hitting 20 points better than the white, baseball is through with him—*forever*. More than anything, this lets the black athlete know that organized baseball does not consider him an equal. There are almost no Negroes among baseball's front-office personnel; there is no Negro manager, and there is only one Negro coach (Jim Gilliam of the Dodgers).

"I guess black people are just too dumb to be in front offices," says Earl Wilson, who won 22 games for Detroit in 1967. "I guess we don't have any knowledge of the game. People say wait five or ten years and it will happen. Well, man, I can't wait. It has to happen now. Strip those twenty-two wins off me and who am I? Just another black man."

Says Pittsburgh's Roberto Clemente: "They're always asking can the colored player do it; do this, do that.

They never ask the white player. They just give him the coaching job."

"I have to watch out for myself when I'm playing," says the Cardinals' Bob Gibson. "When I quit, nobody will come up to me and ask me if I want to be the general manager."

Black players repeatedly cite Bill White of the Phillies as a Negro capable of being a major league manager. "A lot of people have thrown my name around as the first Negro manager," says White. "So far, I haven't seen any club owner throw it around."

Former Negro players speak on this subject quite openly, in part because they have nothing to lose. Wes Covington, who spent 12 years in the major leagues, points out an aspect of baseball's problem that is different from professional football or basketball. For the most part, the Negro baseball player has little education to fall back upon when he has to start job hunting.

"Society needs an educated man," says Covington. "There is no tie between baseball owners and colleges. Baseball had better find ways to give its young Negro players the incentive to go to college. This is a contribution that baseball must consider. If it doesn't, the good Negro athletes won't be in baseball a few years from now. They'll go into other sports."

Larry Doby has even stronger and more urgent feelings on the subject. Normally Doby is a good-natured man, quick to laugh, friendly. His insurance agency business card says " 'Major League' Financial Planning." Dressed in his somber suit and regimental striped tie, he looks like a successful businessman. But all Doby ever really wanted was to stay in baseball. He was the American League's Jackie Robinson, and he hoped base- **183** ball would find a place for him. But baseball did not.

"Baseball has done a lot for the Negro," says Doby, "but the Negro has done more for baseball. Black players have meant gold for baseball owners. I drew a lot of people into Cleveland in those days. I was surprised about two things. Surprised I ever got a chance to play in the big leagues and more surprised I didn't get a chance to stay in when I was through playing. After all, I was a pioneer. It doesn't make sense to me that an insurance company would give me the chance to prove I could handle a job, but baseball wouldn't even let me try.

"I wouldn't go out of my way to go back now. When I think of the way things were, I wonder how we did it. I remember sliding into second base and the fielder spitting tobacco juice in my face, and I just walked away. *I walked away.* They'd shout at you: 'You dirty black so and so!' There's no way to walk away from that, but I did. I didn't have a fight until 1957. Charlie Neal had one in Brooklyn about the same time. I guess we celebrated our independence."

Much of the personal racial animosity that Larry Doby remembers is gone in baseball now. The friction between white and black players today often comes off the field in the area of economics, which is the whole point in pro sports.

Black professional athletes swear that the color of their skin consistently costs them money, and when the white establishment points to Willie Mays and his $125,000 salary the Negroes answer, "Keep on pointing," and it is not very long before there is no one left to point out. Frank Robinson of the Baltimore Orioles figures that the color of his skin has cost him a minimum of $50,000 in salaries alone through the years. The San Francisco Giants have raised the knack of signing non-whites almost to an art form. In the same period that a California white boy named Mike McCormick got a $60,-000 bonus, a Negro named Orlando Cepeda was signing for $500. Giants' owner Horace Stoneham paid $350 for Jim Ray Hart's signature, $500 for Willie McCovey, $500 for Felipe Alou and $4,000 for Juan Marichal.

The black players also find themselves far down on the endorsement scale. One wonders if it could really be true that the sight of a black athlete's face beaming out of a billboard advertising "Okay Cola" would only send the white folks racing to the store for Coca-Cola or Pepsi, or that white buyers would rather fight than switch to a cigarette brand endorsed by a black. "I had a good season in 1967," says Earl Wilson of the Detroit Tigers, "but did my twenty-two wins get me any endorsements? Hell, no! Black people use all the products —except maybe Brylcreem—but we still don't get to endorse anything."

Roberto Clemente of the Pittsburgh Pirates has long been in the superstar category, but his income from endorsements does not reflect his status. "I can make money from cheap products," he says, "but I won't do it. I don't want to advertise just to advertise." He says that a Chicago firm approached him a few years ago to endorse a soft drink and offered him $2,500. "I tell them, 'Okay, I'll do it, but I want $10,000, the same as you pay a white player.' " According to Clemente, the offer was raised to $3,000 but he turned it down.

After he won the triple batting crown in 1966 and was unanimously named the American League's Most Valuable Player, the Orioles' superstar Frank Robinson sat back and waited for the commercial offers to roll in. At the least he figured he would pick up an extra $20,-000 to $30,000 over the winter. By the time the 1967 spring-training season rolled around, Robinson had made a total of one TV appearance and two $500 speaking engagements. When he asked his agent why they had done so little business, the agent said, "Look, they don't want you, and there's nothing I can do about it."

By comparison, Carl Yastrzemski of the Boston Red Sox estimates his 1967 MVP award will be worth about $200,000 over a three-year period. At one point, he was asking a $1,500 to $2,000 fee to attend a baseball writers' dinner in Chicago. When the writers balked, Yastrzemski skipped the dinner. Frank Robinson went— for expenses only.

Of the three major team sports, professional basketball has moved the closest to integration—since half its players are white and half are black it mathematically represents the ultimate in integration—but even in basketball there is more of an uneasy truce than equality. Because the Negro so dominates the sport, the old racial attitudes are kept well in check, but they are there and they die slowly.

Soon after Willie Naulls came to the St. Louis Hawks from UCLA in 1956 he found there was a banquet for the team at a country club and he was the only one not invited. He went straight to the airport to go home. "But then I decided it was easier to quit than to stay, so I stayed. A couple of weeks later I was traded, and things began going right."

Sihugo Green remembers that when he came to the Hawks he was told to "just play defense for the Big **186** Three—Pettit, Hagan and Lovellette. In my first game

I hit my first four shots, and I never got back in that night. The coach said I didn't fit into the system."

Walter Dukes recalls that when he joined the Detroit Pistons in the 1950s, "Blacks could not be shooters, because it was the white fans who supported the game. The whites were the scorers. I was the rebounder and feeder. The plays were set up for the whites to score. Even though in my early years I had a good shooting percentage, I was forced to specialize in rebounding and chasing, to the point that I was constantly in foul trouble.

"The press began to write about me as if I was some kind of clown—the press tends to do this with Negro ballplayers. I remember once the front office sent me to the wrong city for a game, and the press made me out to be an idiot." In basketball circles that unfortunate image has stuck to Dukes to this day. Since he now has a law degree, a master's degree in business administration and an international business based on a travel agency, it is unlikely that Dukes was ever an idiot. But the world of pro basketball always tended to assume he was.

The indisputable talent of the Negro basketball player is slowly forcing changes in such attitudes. NBA franchises have never been strong. Winning is vital, and it takes Negroes to win. The economics of the matter cannot be escaped. Red Auerbach knew this and showed the way by using many black starters on the Boston Celtics. Eventually he made a move that no other major sport has dared: he appointed a militant Negro, Bill Russell, to succeed him as coach. "Because of this," says Dukes, "pro basketball has begun to realize what competition really means—fair play and a fair chance."

Maybe so, but a lot of Negro players are not as certain as Dukes that attitudes have materially changed. To use the baseball image, they still know that they have to hit 20 points higher than the whites.

Can there be such a thing as a professional sports unit in America that works together and lives together without racial discrimination, or is the problem of prejudice as virulent in sport as it seems to be in every other aspect of American society? The overwhelming evidence is that pro sport has not been able to lead the way to new attitudes or new accommodations, that it has found no way to divorce itself from the dreary intolerance seen in all the other avenues of American life.

There are two possible exceptions. One is the Celtics, a small squad led by a dynamic, outspoken black under conditions that hardly would permit internal racism. The other is more interesting, because it involves a sport where Negroes are still in the minority, and a team whose boss is white—which means it more closely approximates conditions in the country as a whole. That team is the Green Bay Packers.

Whenever racial questions are discussed by NFL players, the Packers are mentioned. In a league beset with racial confrontations, the Packer players get along. Success has something to do with this; a winner always finds life more pleasant than a loser. But more to the point is the attitude of the Packers' remarkable Vince Lombardi.

Aided by the fact that Green Bay is an isolated community with no significant Negro population of its own, Lombardi has insisted that his Packers be a family. "If you're black or white, you're a part of the family," he says. He will permit nothing that is antithetical to this

188

idea. "We make no issue over a man's color. I just won't tolerate anybody in this organization making it an issue. We respect every man's dignity, black or white. I won't stand for any movements or groups on our ball club. If anything is bothering any of our players, we settle whatever it is right away. If we find something that doesn't fit in with the Packers, we lick it before it starts."

There is nothing in this particular credo that every coach in the country would not repeat with equal earnestness. The difference is that Lombardi means it, and he enforces his belief as only Lombardi can.

"I can't think of a single racial incident we have had," says Willie Wood. "Green Bay is such a small town that you can't have a difference with a player, because you wouldn't have anywhere to go. A lot of credit in past years goes to Em Tunnell [a black defensive back] and Paul Hornung. Tunnell was a natural leader. The players took to him. He and Hornung were almost inseparable, and Hornung knew no color. Lombardi has picked men for the Packers who are bigger than any little racial hatred. We go over to Bart Starr's for dinner. When new players came they saw how Starr from Alabama and Hornung from Kentucky and the others acted. So there was only one way for the new fellows to act, no matter where they were from."

"The important thing," says linebacker Dave Robinson, "is that everybody gets equal treatment. Any time you feel some hostility over something that has happened, you soon find out that the same treatment is being dished out to the whites. It never enters my mind that I'm being chewed out because I'm a Negro."

"No," says Lombardi, "we haven't had any problems. And we don't anticipate any."

189

11

In professional sports, winning is everything. To everybody even faintly interested in a pro team—coaches, players, fans—the concept is so self-evident that it hardly needs to be stated. Yet on the promising St. Louis Cardinal football team of 1967, the divisive poison of racial prejudice made a logical absurdity of the whole point of professional athletics. The Cardinals' record was a mediocre 6-7-1, and bias—actively fostered by a few white players, tolerated or unsuspected by some of the coaches—had much to do with their failures. When the resentment of black players against what they felt to be slurs and mistreatment finally broke into the open, some of the poison was drained, but by then the dismal season was well advanced.

There were early signs of the trouble, hints that the Cardinal management might have picked up, had they viewed all their players as human beings. On one out-of-town trip a front-office staffer was sitting in a Cardinal plane when an oversized lineman squeezed into the next seat and began babbling. "Do you have a soul?" the lineman said. "Well, I know I have one. I've been on earth before." The Cardinals had won that afternoon's game against the Washington Redskins, and no one else on the flight home was engaged in deep discussions about reincarnation or life after death.

The player rambled on. "A long, long time ago I was here and I was a cockroach," he said, "and people pushed me around and stepped on me and finally killed me. Then I was reincarnated as a buffalo, and people shot me and I died." The lineman paused. "And then I came back as an American Negro," he said. *"I can't win no way!"* Later, when the excitement started, the front-office man was to remember that remark vividly.

Others were to recall the time a group of black Cardinals strolled into the dressing room with medallions dangling from their necks. Some of them were young players, still largely unproved men—linebacker Jamie Rivers and running back Roy Shivers and defensive end Fred Heron; but there were also such seasoned players as Bobby Reynolds, a first-string tackle, and cornerback Bobby Williams. At first sight of this black contingent descending upon the dressing room, the other players merely gawked. Then the acknowledged leader of the team's white supremacy cell, an outspoken man with a quick mind and a caustic wit, stepped up to Williams. He looked the 26-year-old player up and down and finally said, "What the hell's that around your neck? You trying to strangle yourself?"

Williams said jokingly, "Man, that's black power!"

The white player groaned and rolled his eyes at the ceiling. "Bobby," he said, "if you're indicative of black power, and all the other niggers are as smart as you, we whites will never have anything to worry about!"

Ernie McMillan, the 260-pound offensive tackle in his seventh year with the club, sat in front of his locker shaking his head dolefully. Later he said to a friend, "One of the white boys asked, 'What are those things?' and Bobby said, 'black power,' and the white player believed him. Now how naïve can a guy be? Those aren't black power medallions. Did you ever see one around

Stokely Carmichael's neck or Rap Brown's? And yet some of these white players are naïve enough to believe the first thing that's told 'em!"

Such incidents, each too small in itself to become a *casus belli*, accumulated with the steady irritating effect of a leaky faucet. They created an atmosphere in which the normal banter and horseplay of athletes—the bench jockeying and the hollering and shoving of the locker room—were corroded by petty racism. The result: cumulative frustration, hostility—and finally, an explosion.

The situation on the Cardinals team may or may not be worse than that on other NFL teams. Almost every team, for example, has a cell of white racists like the one on the Cardinals, one that geographical origin does not explain. On the Cardinals, the white racist group was dominated by a player from the North, and several of the team's most outspoken anti-Negroes were from above the Mason-Dixon line. Says Prentice Gautt, a former Cardinal running back who has been hired as assistant football coach at the University of Missouri: "Somebody said to me once, 'You must have a hard core of red-necks on the Cardinals.' I said, 'You deal in understatement!'"

"Two or three bad racists polarized the whole team," says a white Cardinal who has managed to remain apart from the clique. "The problem was that the leader of the racist clique was intelligent. He was a natural spokesman for bigots, and because he was so witty and such a good ballplayer, he commanded respect and he influenced new players far beyond normal."

"The haters come in all shapes and sizes," says Willis Crenshaw, the handsome first-string running back whose hometown is St. Louis. "A few of them have

192

these quick tongues, yes, but some of them are just plain stupid, too. If it wasn't for football, they'd be zeroes. We have one hater who posed as a good Christian boy. It's a hoax. He thinks he can counsel Negroes, but at the same time, he's no different from the other racists on the team. After we made our complaints and the whole thing came out into the open, this guy went around saying that it came as a big surprise to him. Sure, it did. The reason he was surprised is he thought you were *supposed* to treat Negroes bad. That's the way it's done where he comes from."

Roy Shivers, the tough little runner from Utah State who signed for an estimated $300,000 in bonus and salaries, speaks bitterly of the general situation on the Cardinals. "Every white player wants to be a coach," Shivers says, "and he practices on the Negroes. Every time a Negro player makes a mistake on this ball club he's got two coaches and six players clustering around him to tell him what he did wrong. This situation comes straight down from the coaching staff and the front office. Now, you don't go around doing like this! We even have certain ballplayers that'll cuss the coach out, but let a Negro do something like that and see how long he'll stay here! There's a double standard any way you look. And that's the history of this team, and for all I know, the other teams too. It used to be *really* bad on the Cardinals. Veterans like Prentice Gautt— they can talk for hours on what was done to them on this ball club. But I don't think it's *that* much better right now."

Shivers has had to take especially harsh treatment from the white supremacy forces on the Cardinals, partially because he is married to a white woman. His position has been made all the more difficult because he is on the punt-return team; he is one of those stoic individuals who must stand all alone in the cold fall air and wait for a long kick to descend to earth while a ton of opposing flesh charges down the field and thousands of fans await the fumble. "I realize I should be a professional and stay loose out there," Shivers says, "but every Negro player on this team is tense. In my rookie season I returned a punt, and after I was tackled, this big white player of ours grabs me by the shoulders and he hollers things like 'You little bastard, you don't even know how to follow blocking.' "

In the 1967 season's opening game before a crowd of 40,000 fans at Busch Stadium in St. Louis, Shivers fumbled just before the half. "The Giants tried a field goal and missed it," Shivers recalls, "and my fumble didn't hurt us. And then comes the gun for the half, and the snide remarks begin. 'Hold onto the ball, you little punk!' Stuff like that! It kept up all through the halftime. Now, I'm a professional. Nobody needs to tell me when I make a mistake. Honest to God, I know I'm a Negro and I'm not supposed to have any brains and I'm supposed to be some kind of an inferior animal, but, honest to God, I *knew* I had fumbled! *I already knew it!* We're running out on the field for the second half, and they're still on me. And it was on my mind something awful not to fumble again, and I fumbled the first chance I got. In the locker room that's all you heard about. And after something like this I'd go home and sit up at night and wonder: Am I bad? Did I deserve what they said? You know, going crazy is a thin line. A lot of times I come home to my apartment and look at the four walls and get to thinking how this stuff doesn't

194

seem real, and I begin to wonder about myself. For the first time in my life, I'm beginning to wonder."

Willis Crenshaw is now a regular on the Cardinals, unlike the struggling Shivers, but he has been through some of the same agonies. "I think I had about five fumbles in the 1966 season," he says, "but I was benched for the rest of the season when I fumbled twice against Chicago in our eighth game. And from then on the white players were on me about fumbling. I was ostracized, and it took me a long time to get over the tension from that. When you do get a chance to get back in there and show what you can do, you're so tense that you just mess up anyway. So what's the result? The result is that the Cardinals have paid the highest salaries and bonuses and put together the best personnel in pro football, and we don't win anything!"

Now and then Crenshaw finds himself wondering whose side the Cardinal red-necks are on. "Some of them can get the old tension started even *before* the game," he says. "Like, one day I showed up in the dressing room fifty-five minutes before the game started. We're supposed to be there an hour before the whistle, but I'm the kind of ballplayer that hates to sit around waiting. I get overly nervous, so I like to just come in and dress and go out on the field and play. So I come in five minutes late and this big white player tromps over and he says, 'If you'd think more about the games, maybe we'd do a lot better than we're doing.'

"I says, 'What do you mean by that?'

"He says, 'You think you can walk in here any time you want to.' And he's talking at the top of his lungs, and everybody in the place can hear this, including the coaches. But nobody says a word. So I says, 'Hey, man, you're a player. Do you think you can chew me out just because you feel like it? If somebody's gonna chew me out, it's gonna be the coach.'

"And he got mad. He started hollering all kinds of junk. You can imagine how we felt when we went out to play the game. But this guy's a particularly big offender. He was doing stuff like that all the time. Once, one of our black players clipped somebody on a punt return and this white guy ran off our bench and hollered, 'Don't you ever do that again!' And he ran his own teammate off the field! Where are the coaches when stuff like this is going on? They're sitting there watching."

Says Johnny Roland, 1966 Rookie of the Year and the big spike in the Cardinal backfield: "Some of those white guys can ruin a ballplayer, a *good* ballplayer. A guy like Charlie Bryant deserves some special handling— he's a very nervous individual, one of these guys who goes to sleep at midnight and gets up at 5 a.m. You know the kind. Being nervous, he makes mistakes. Not that he doesn't know the plays, or that he isn't bright, but he gets excited. Now, this could all be overcome, but instead, some of the white players ride him and make him more nervous, and it's like a chain reaction."

"They holler at Charlie that he's dumb," says cornerback Bobby Williams, who also is a favorite target of Cardinal racists, "and Charlie gets all shook up and makes another mistake and they holler, 'Dumb! Dumb! Dumb!' at him. And then they figure they can treat him like dirt. One time he's playing on the punting team and he got hurt pretty bad, and one of the white guys ran out on the field and stood over him and hollered, 'Get up, you son of a bitch, you're not hurt! Get off the field!' I said, 'Wait a minute, man, the guy's hurt!' I said, 'Stay down, Charlie, let the referee call a time out. If you're hurting, don't be jumping right up.' I got me *some* look from that white player!"

According to the racists on the team, Negroes like Bobby Williams and Charlie Bryant are troublemakers who would be cut from any other squad. "We kept ten Negroes around here last year that don't even belong in football," says the leader of the group, the man with the great talent and twisted views and sharp tongue. "They say they're being prejudiced against, and yet I can name you ten of those guys—and I'll put fifty thousand dollars in escrow tomorrow that if any one of them ever stars for a team in the NFL, you can have the money. That's how bad they are! Some of them couldn't make my college team. And yet these guys are in the upper one per cent of the per capita income of all Negroes, and if this is the way they're going to act with all that money, complaining all the time, just think what a miserable place this country's gonna be when the other shines catch up."

This argument—that only the Cardinals' marginal players make complaints—ignores the fact that every Negro on the team approved the letter that finally brought the gripes into the open. "It's true that I've been treated pretty good on the club," says Johnny Roland, "but I got eyes! I could see what they were doing to the other guys. And I had to say to myself, 'Suppose you weren't Rookie of the Year? Suppose they could just reach out and replace you real easy? How would they be treating you?' I'd be getting what guys like Fred Heron were getting."

Fred Heron played at San Jose State as a defensive tackle, and was drafted by the Packers, who traded **197** him to St. Louis in 1966. Some of his black teammates feel that Heron has the talent to be an All-League defensive lineman, but so far he has failed to live up to any portion of his promise.

"These things are hard to figure," says Willis Crenshaw, "but I'm willing to bet that most of Fred's trouble is in his mind. He has a tendency to get excited, and when he does, he stutters. I'm kind of touchy about this myself, because I have a speech defect, kind of a lisp, and I'm conscious of defects in others. I mean, you should consider yourself fortunate, and try to help people with defects. But one day we were all sitting at a meeting in training camp and one of the coaches was making up a list of who wanted steak and who wanted eggs for the pregame meal, and when he got to Fred, he said, 'Fred, do you want steak or eggs?' and Fred stood up and he was all excited, because he was a rookie, and he couldn't get it out. And everybody started cracking up. From then on some of the white players would go up to Fred and say, 'Hey, Fred, how do you like your eggs?' and then they'd laugh themselves silly. Now I know this isn't necessarily a racial thing. Anyway, it's hard to show that it is. It's more like something that permeates the whole Cardinal team. The Cardinals like to pick on the frailties of individuals, whether it's their color or their speech or whatever. And then it goes from that into outright nastiness. I mean, if they can kid a guy about a speech defect and get away with it, why not start bullying him too?"

Once, the Cardinals were showering after one of their losses, and Fred Heron made the mistake of flushing a toilet; the effect was to draw off cold water from the system and turn the shower into a momentary red-hot spray. A white player jumped out of the shower and called Heron a "black son of a bitch." Heron says, "This wasn't the first time he'd called me a black something-or-other, but now he's not only saying that, he's acting like he wants to fight! I couldn't get it through my head what he was hollering about. Excuse me, but I'd always been taught that you were supposed to flush toilets after you use them. So I tried to reason with him. I said, 'Look, you don't have to cuss at me, and especially, you didn't have to say what you said.' But he kept right on. The coaches were there too. They heard every word of it, but as usual they didn't make a move. So finally I told him to watch his mouth or I'd have to bust him and I turned around and walked away, and as I was walking I could hear all this abuse behind me. But I tried to forget about it, to overlook it. Everybody's upset when you lose a game."

One day the same white player who had abused Fred Heron in the shower took Bobby Williams aside and said, "Hey, Bobby, you know what Coach Drulis called you this morning? A nigger." The angered Williams ran into the coach's office and confronted him with the charge, which was promptly denied, and after talking to everyone who had been with the coach that morning, Williams concluded that the white player had only been trying to stir up trouble. "That was his idea of a good laugh," Williams says.

The effect of such bigotry on a team like the Cardinals is to force a lot of apathetic whites across the line into racism, and to divide the team sharply down the middle. As of the end of the 1967 season, there were eight or 10 ardent racists on the Cardinal roster, and another eight or 10 whose hearts were not in it, but who were bowing to the pressure from the right. The Negroes speak of this as "secondary pressure" and tend to look down on these influenced players as spineless. "Secondary pressure is a big thing on this team," says Willis Crenshaw. "Here's how it works. We had two Negro rookies, Ted Wheeler and Jamie Rivers, and they were real good friends with two white players. In fact, they were all gonna be roommates together. But when they got settled in St. Louis the haters put so much pressure on these guys that it all ended. You can see this secondary pressure even in the Sideliners, our wives' club. At the beginning of each season, the new white wives are always friendly to the Negro wives, but as the season goes on they become more and more aloof."

Some of the lily-white members of the Sideliners were shocked during the 1967 season when they looked up from their drinks to see the extremely black Bobby Williams doing the boogaloo with the extremely white Kit Gambrell, the lissome wife of split end Billy Gambrell. The Gambrells are Southerners—Billy is from Georgia and his wife from South Carolina—but they treat people as individuals, and on at least one occasion Billy has been close to a fistfight with white teammates over the subject of race on the Cardinals. His wife tells the story of the dance: "It was at the Falstaff Inn, where the team goes to relax, and Bobby went out on the floor in front of people and said, 'Come on, Kit, let's dance,' and I certainly wasn't about to embarrass him. I felt that if my husband didn't object—which he certainly didn't—and Bobby Williams had always treated me like a lady, well, I certainly wouldn't embarrass him. And you know how the boogaloo and the stomp and these modern dances are; you don't even *touch*

200

your partner. But I was shocked when I saw what was happening when we started to dance. You could see the huddles gathering and people whispering together. They were getting upset! It hurt me so much for people to act so small."

Willis Crenshaw remembers the scene; indeed, it was one of the dramatic high points of the Cardinals' lackluster season. "There was no roll of drums, or anything like that," Crenshaw says, "and nobody hollered 'Stop the music!' but everybody knew what was going on. The tension filled the place like a low cloud."

Bobby Williams did nothing to ease matters when he thanked Mrs. Gambrell for the dance and strolled over to the wife of one of the most prejudiced players to ask her for the next dance. "She said she was just too tired," Williams says, chuckling at his own audacity. "My wife was there; she got a big kick out of it."

Other incidents involving race and sex have not been so funny to the black Cardinals. One white woman who was seen sitting in a nightclub with a Negro player was called "nigger lover" to her face by a white player. Not many years ago a white member of the Cardinal staff told a white maid at training camp that she should stop seeing one of the Negro players. He told her she would be better off to date somebody like— well, er—himself. The maid compromised; she dated both men, and for the rest of the season she kept the black player informed about the white man's racial outbursts. "That was a *great* help for team solidarity," says Johnny Roland. "It was like *Peyton Place*."

A white player bristles at the nerve of Negroes who tell such tales. "They say things like that about whites and then they want our respect!" he says. "Well, they **201** won't have our respect as long as they keep getting caught with white women. To me, that's the worst offense there is—dating white girls. They'll take a white girl out, and then they'll stand up in a team meeting and say, 'We demand your respect.' And our Southern guys just hate 'em for it!"

Sometimes this feeling is made explicit. Last year when the Cardinals played in Washington, D.C., Roy Shivers bumped into a girl he had known in college, at Utah State. "We were old friends," Shivers says. "She'd sort of felt sorry for me in college, and sometimes she practically kept me from starving. I knew her fiancé, and it was perfectly all right with everybody when I took her out to dinner in the restaurant of the Dupont Plaza Hotel. That's where the team was staying, and I wasn't trying to hide from anybody. Well, after dinner we were sitting out in the lobby talking and a couple of the Cardinal coaches came by and gave us the funny look and started laughing. The next thing I knew, one of the older Negro players came to me and said, 'The coach wants you to cool it, be a bit more discreet.' I said, 'Can't I have friends?' "

On Willis Crenshaw's first road trip with the Cardinals, he had a long conversation with a stewardess on the St. Louis-Dallas run. "Just before we landed," Crenshaw recalls, "this girl said to me, 'Give me a call.' Well, when we got off the plane one of the white guys cornered me and said, 'If I was you, I wouldn't try to make a white girl in front of the team.' You could tell he was trying to keep his voice down, pretend like he really didn't care, but he was puffing and he was red as a beet in the face. I said, 'Make a white girl? Who was trying to make a white girl?' He says, 'If I was you, I'd

202

be smarter than that.' Then he started to huff and puff and get all worked up about it. So I finally said, 'Well, I don't want to cause any trouble on the team. I'm just a rookie, and if you think it's detrimental for me to talk to a stewardess, I'll just cool it!' I know of several cases where the white players got themselves lined up with Negro girls. So what? Am I supposed to get all excited and tell them to cool it, that it's detrimental to the team?"

When the Cardinals get off the plane after road trips, the racial divisions between players are aggravated by certain St. Louisans whose connection with the team is unofficial. People in the cities where professional athletes play their home games are generally proud of their teams, and some go out of their way to help. One such active fan is a St. Louis merchant who sells meat to Cardinal players at a discount—but the policy is operated to favor whites only. "He runs a place where the white players used to go and get fifty dollars worth of meat for fifteen dollars," says Prentice Gautt. "A long time ago the meat man sent one of the white ballplayers back to tell us that Negroes weren't wanted there. He said we were hurting his business. I think it's all straightened out now, but I still don't think he gives the Negroes as much discount as he gives the whites."

Gautt's former teammates agree. Says Ernie McMillan: "You wouldn't catch me buying meat from that man, even though he *will* sell it to us if we put in our orders by telephone. Abe Woodson used to go down there, and once he added it all up and found out he was paying the full price!" Bobby Williams says one of the team's Negroes put in a large order and compared the discount against the one given the same day to a white player. "The white guy was getting a hell of a lot off, almost getting the meat free," says Williams. "The black discount was three per cent. And then around Christmastime you'll see the white players in the locker room collecting money for a present for this meat guy, and another present for a guy who sells hunting equipment at a discount—to whites only. One day a white player comes up to me and he says, 'We're collecting for the meat man.' I said, 'For who?' He named the guy and I said, 'Who's he?' The white player said, 'He's the guy who gives us the meat.' I said, 'Gives *who* the meat? He don't give *me* no meat.' So the white guy says, 'Well, then, you don't have to give anything.' I says, 'Thank you very much.' But wouldn't you think they'd have a list right up on the bulletin board: who gives discounts to members of the Cardinals, and how much and all that? No, it's all secret stuff, and it's mostly all white."

"It's a free country," says Ernie McMillan, who came as close to being leader of the black Cardinals as anyone, after Prentice Gautt left. "If they want to give special deals to the whites, that's their business. But there's no unity on a football team when some of the players will accept favors that are denied to another because of his color. You can say, 'So what? You don't have to give me any meat.' But it eats away at you. It takes a hell of a guy not to be bothered by something like that. He's a member of the team, but he can't take part."

Says a white member of the team, one of the handful who refuse to do business with the white-only discounters: "This looks like nothing, I know, but the white guys are making a big mistake. If a merchant wants to give a certain gift to a favorite player that he admires and that he has come to know personally, fine! But when color becomes the sole criterion of these favors, then the Negro players are absolutely right in feeling that their white teammates are letting them down."

According to the dozen or so Negroes on the Cardinal roster, their coaches also had let them down. "In fact," says Johnny Roland, "the coaches are maybe more to blame, because they set a tone that the white racist guys just follow. Some of the coaches treat us like animals, so why shouldn't the players do the same?" Says Gautt: "We had a Negro player who was always told that he didn't know his plays. The coaches' overall attitude was that he just wasn't smart enough. Maybe he was and maybe he wasn't, but some of us got the impression that this was just because he was a Negro. *Dumb* is the way he was made to feel. And soon the rest of the team was treating him the same way."

To hear the Negro Cardinals tell about it, the prejudice begins even before the team hits the locker room. "There are definite signs of quotas and definite signs that players are stacked at certain positions," says Johnny Roland. "It isn't enough for a Negro to be good to make this team. He's got to be better than good. Of course, every team has the same rule: 'Be tough on rookies!' But when the rookie is a Negro, something else comes out secondarily—to be a little bit tougher."

The case of Ed McQuarters continues to baffle the black Cardinals. McQuarters was a reserve defensive tackle, and he impressed his Negro teammates highly. "He was a whole lot better than lots of other tackles I'd seen," says Bobby Williams, "and at Oklahoma he was one of the greatest linemen *anybody'd* ever seen." Mc-

Quarters had the quickness and instincts of a defensive tackle, but he was ill-equipped for the position to which he was switched: defensive end. "He was only six foot one," says Ernie McMillan, "and he didn't have a feeling for the position. He was shorter than every guy he played against. The guy would straighten up and Ed would be lost. At end he didn't have a chance, trying to take the job from great players like Joe Robb and Don Brumm. But in the middle of the line his quickness paid off, and he could work."

McQuarters was cut from the squad in his second year, and ended up playing in the Canadian League, where he was named Most Outstanding Lineman for 1967. "Don't ask me," says McMillan, "I can't explain it. Even some of the most prejudiced white players said they didn't understand that one."

Says head coach Charley Winner, "We just didn't feel that Ed was good enough. He hadn't shown us anything. He didn't seem to have the temperament. It was a tossup which guy we kept, and we let Ed go. Ed was a real fine guy, no troublemaker, but I don't regret letting him go. This is the sort of thing that will come up because Ed is a Negro. Nothing has been said about the white boys we let go who were in pretty much the same situation."

By itself, the case of Ed McQuarters proves neither that the Cardinals have a quota system nor that Negroes are stacked into certain positions while white players get their jobs automatically, as is so often the case on college football teams. But it is suggestive of both possibilities. As one white Cardinal says, "The front office has nobody but itself to blame if people run around accusing them of cutting Ed McQuarters for racial reasons.

If there weren't so many other racial things going on here, the thought wouldn't have entered anybody's head. It's possible the Negroes are only being touchy. But who the hell can blame them for being touchy the way they're treated around here?"

"All we ask is open competition for positions," says Willis Crenshaw, "and it hasn't been open. If a Negro ballplayer makes a mistake and there's a white ballplayer pushing him for the position, they make the switch right away. But if it's the other way around, the white stays in. Two of our white defensive players, Pat Fischer and Jimmy Burson, were getting passes thrown over them all season, and they were heavily criticized for it, even though it wasn't their fault, because Robb and Brumm, our defensive ends, were injured and we didn't have enough outside pressure on the quarterback. But people were openly demanding that something be done about Burson and Fischer, and all the time we had an outstanding Negro cornerback ready to start: Bobby Williams, a hell of a player. And for the whole season, they kept starting the two white guys. It wasn't enough that Bobby was good; he had to be fantastic!"

Bobby Williams is a special bone of contention on the St. Louis Cardinals, and one may be excused for supposing that he too would be in the Canadian League were it not for his exceptional ability. "From the beginning, Bobby brought problems," says Johnny Roland. "He likes to hit. And some of our ends would be coming out on their patterns in practice and *whack!* Bobby'd dump them. Some of the older ballplayers didn't like this, and they started calling him 'Cassius.' And he'd say, 'Okay, go ahead calling me Cassius, but when you come out on this side, expect to get hit!' "

"Sonny Randle didn't like it, for one," Williams says, "and I can understand it, now. I just wanted to make the team, and I figured if I could knock some of the big names down I'd have a better chance. But the coach told me to lighten up, and now I know he was right."

"But you had the feeling they were just laying for Bobby, waiting to get back at him," Johnny Roland says. "Then during the regular season Bobby began to have problems with this complicated defense that coach Chuck Drulis had set up, and some days in practice he might mess up a coverage or something and Drulis and some of the white ballplayers would get to talking about him. They'd see him playing cards in the locker room and they'd say, 'You should be studying your play book, not playing cards.'"

Such a criticism may have been justified, but it was not isolated. Little by little the word was spread among the white team members that Bobby Williams was stupid. No one is more aware of the canard than Williams himself, who has his own explanations. "In the first place," he says, "Coach Drulis seems to have the idea that all Negroes are stupid. I was just a little more stupid than the others. That's the way he looks at it. And when I'd get out on the field, he'd say, 'Bobby, don't you know your plays?' and 'Bobby, don't you know this, and don't you know that?' He'd say, 'Bobby, didn't you ever learn this in school?' Some people seem to have the idea that they can say anything they want to a Negro, that Negroes don't have feelings.

"Then it got so I couldn't do anything right for Coach Drulis. Later on he told me he was just getting on me to help me make the team, but somehow I felt he was on me just for the fun of it. One day we were having a question-and-answer session and they showed a film and I asked to say something and Drulis said, 'Shut up or you'll be kicked off the team.' But the white guys were talking all they wanted to."

According to Prentice Gautt, such threats by Cardinal coaches had to be taken seriously. Gautt had sat in on one of those coaching sessions years before and listened as another Negro player talked back to a Cardinal coach. "If he were white, he'd still be on the team," Gautt said. "He was playing first-string defense, and the guy who took his position shouldn't have made the ball club. Maybe it got back to the quota, I don't know. Maybe it worked out better for the quota if they could get rid of the Negro and play a white player, which is what they did." Willie West, the player the Cardinals lost, now is a defensive star for the Miami Dolphins, of the AFL.

Chuck Drulis is a craggy-faced, tough-talking defensive coach who, along with men like Tom Landry of the Dallas Cowboys and George Allen of the Los Angeles Rams, is regarded as one of the finest defensive minds in pro football. The Cardinal players who dislike him the most heartily are of one mind about his talents. "That's one reason it hurts so much when he treats you bad," says Bobby Williams, "because as a defensive coach, he's the greatest." Drulis' voice remains on the edge of hoarseness all through the football season, a symptom of one of his stocks-in-trade: shouting at players à la Vince Lombardi.

"Chuck is a rough, tough character," says head coach Charley Winner. "He's a good old professional football player that's got a great football mind. He's a straight-talker. He doesn't give you any window dressing. He talks right out. He might say to a player, 'You dumb bastard!' and he doesn't mean a thing by it. But I can see how a Negro player might misunderstand his gruffness."

It is also possible that Charley Winner might have misunderstood Chuck Drulis, and Drulis misunderstood himself. Drulis says, "When this racial trouble came up, I was hurt more inside than anything in the last ten years. Deep down in my heart, I don't think I ever did nothing to them to my knowledge. If I did, I didn't know about it. I told Coach Winner: 'I am not prejudiced and I have never acted in a prejudiced way.' I even used to say that one of our big problems last year was that we needed a good colored cornerman." Why a good *colored* cornerman? According to Drulis, "The colored ballplayers want to create a problem. They use race as an excuse. Your good guys don't cause these problems, it's your mediocre guys. Some of these mediocre players aren't as active in their thinking as some of the other ballplayers."

There are white Cardinals who have entertained their own doubts about Drulis' freedom from prejudice, although they seem to feel that he is not much different from the typical old-line pro football coach. Says one: "He has that thing against black linebackers and centers and guards, but who in the league doesn't? He doesn't think they're smart enough to play positions like that. I was told that as soon as I came on the ball club." (Says Drulis about Negro linebackers: "I don't have any. What am I supposed to do, make one?")

The black players talk about Drulis. "I've heard people say in his behalf that he hollers at *everybody*, black and white," says Willis Crenshaw. "But that doesn't explain why all the Negroes on the defensive team think he shows prejudice against them. They should know. They have no reason to lie about it."

Says Johnny Roland: "Drulis set the tone for the whole team. When we'd be watching films, one of the assistant offensive coaches would say, 'Look at that big chugabuck lumbering down the field.' And it would always be a Negro he'd say that about. This was an attitude that started with Coach Drulis. He seemed to have a manner of looking down on Negroes. But I doubt if he ever realized he was doing it."

After last year's Pittsburgh game, which resulted in a disappointing 14-14 tie, Drulis tore into Bobby Williams in front of the other players. "I did let them throw two passes over me," Williams says, "and Coach Drulis said it was my fault that we didn't win the game. But they didn't score on those two passes, and then we put in another cornerback, and they scored a touchdown on him, but it was still my fault. The other cornerbacks were getting beat all year and he hardly said anything to them."

Says Drulis: "I might have put Bobby on the ropes a little after the Pittsburgh game, yes, but I do that with everybody else too. But later I had another talk with him and I said, 'Look, Bobby, you think I had something in mind just because you're colored. Now you tell me: Who was the first substitute I put into the ball game the week after the Pittsburgh game, and the week after that, and the week after that?' He said, 'Me.' I said, 'Look, I didn't have to use you. If I had race prejudice in mind I had two whites I could have used. But I used you because I thought that much of you.' I put it right to his face. He never was benched! And he *did* make a couple bad plays in that game. So did a white   **211** player, Jimmy Burson. Burson let them get a touchdown on one pass, and I put him on the ropes too. Bobby's job was to not let a receiver inside, like in the slant pattern, and not only did he let them get inside, but he missed the tackles in both instances and cost us ten or fifteen yards more each time. I bawled him out plenty. But it never entered my mind he was colored. The other coaches wanted to cut him, but I said no."

Drulis' explanation notwithstanding, the black Cardinals felt he had gone far overboard in blaming Williams for the tie that should have been a crucial victory. It was not only a question of the quality of his playing; they felt that by singling out Williams in front of the others Drulis had opened the door to another flood of invective by the team's racists, and it was not long in coming. "Bobby Williams?" said the player who leads the racist cabal. "I'll tell you about him. They say that the average I.Q. of a nigger is eighty-one. Well, you put five Bobby Williamses together and you wouldn't get eighty-one! This guy made six straight mistakes against Pittsburgh and cost us a run at the championship. And this is one of the guys that hollers he's being discriminated against. One of the big instigators." Williams' acknowledged pair of errors had grown to "six straight," and his I.Q. had dwindled almost to zero.

No one is saying who the real "big instigator" was, if indeed there was a *single* "big instigator," but after the Pittsburgh game, the Negro Cardinals began to discuss practical ways to eliminate racism on the football team, and more and more the name of Chuck Drulis began to come up. There was a gentle irony in the fact that one of the cases against the coach from Pennsylvania involved defensive tackle Sam Silas, who once had been known as "Chuck's boy" on the Cardinal defensive team. "If it wasn't for Chuck Drulis, Silas would have been out of the league the day he came here," says a bitter white player. Silas himself admits that "Drulis was in my corner from the beginning. He gave me the first-string tackle job early, and I got the job from a white man. I was his pet."

Like Bobby Williams, Sam Silas is a special case on the Cardinals. A six-foot four-inch 250-pound rock on the defensive line, he has the reputation of being all but immovable when an offensive ballcarrier tries to run over him, and yet he is quick enough on the pass rush. No one seems to object to these qualities in Sam Silas. It is *off* the field that Silas gets under the skin of some of his white teammates. He is that disturbing character, the hard-working, successful Negro. If he lost his pro job tomorrow, Sam Silas would continue breezing along economically. He owns a student dormitory in Carbondale, home of his alma mater, Southern Illinois University. He also owns a small apartment complex. He works for the University as a counselor and for Old Heritage Life Insurance Company as an investment consultant. He is a licensed pilot, and sometimes flies a plane to preseason meetings of the Cardinal staff in St. Louis, one hundred miles northwest of Carbondale. In his spare time, he is working on his doctor's degree in physical education; he hopes to write his dissertation on the *Effects of Ingested Salt on Heart Performance*. On the slightest pretext, Sam Silas will talk you silly about the relationship of salt to the system. He knows his subject, and he knows himself. "I've done quite well outside of football," says Sam, who was brought up in a poor family in Bartow, Florida, "and this doesn't go over so well on the team because it reflects a nigger who is getting above his station."

A charter member of the Cardinals' "hatred" club agrees. "Because he's working on a doctorate," this player says about Silas, "he thinks of himself as one of the aristocratic smart niggers. I think in his doctorate work he's trying to find his way out of the first turn in the rat maze. That's about how smart he is. Tightening barbells for a Ph.D.!"

Inevitably, it has become Sam Silas' lot to be known in certain circles on the St. Louis Cardinal football team as "dumb," "thick-headed," a "stupid nigger." He knows his reputation, and he addresses himself to the subject calmly, methodically and thoroughly. "It is true that certain people have tried to make me feel stupid," he says. "Maybe they don't interpret me correctly. If a person is not explicit with me, then I question him. The only way you'll learn to do your job is to know exactly what's expected. And then I also like to think things through if the entire puzzle doesn't piece itself together, and I *will* ask questions. Maybe some people think I ask too many questions. Or maybe another reason they say I'm stupid is because I've been excelling academically."

Sam Silas has excelled on the football field as well. In 1966, he was named to the Pro-Bowl team, and his big troubles began. Silas refuses to discuss the matter, holding that it is nobody's business but his and the team's. A black teammate tells the story:

"Before he went off to the Pro Bowl, Sam must have told six thousand people that he owed everything to Chuck Drulis, and he wasn't far wrong, either. Never mind his color: Sam was Drulis' boy and everybody knew it. Silas went to the Pro Bowl and his roommate turned out to be Roosevelt Brown. Everybody knows Rosey, and those who don't know him *want* to know him, and his friends come in all colors. And there are times too when the girls flock around Rosey, not to do anything that is unbecoming, but just because they admire him so much. Well, the two of them hit it off real well together, and they hung around together, and the stories started flying about Drulis' boy. Somebody said he and Rosey had been out chasing white girls. The factual basis for that was that Rosey talked to this one white girl a couple of times and the other guys saw her around his place, and another time some white girl fell all over Sam and Rosey when they were walking back to their room. That was the sum total of the chasing.

"Well, when Sam got back to the next Cardinal training camp everything seemed to be different. He certainly wasn't Drulis' boy any more. He'd ask a question and they'd say, 'You never asked questions like *that* before.' If he'd make a mistake on the field, somebody'd say, 'You never played like *that* before.' And one time I heard Drulis say to him, 'I never expected to hear a question like *that* from a candidate for a Ph.D.!' That's the way it was going. Sam was being hazed, like a rookie.

"But he was still the first-string tackle. Then one day Drulis called him in and asked him if it was true he had been chasing white girls with Rosey Brown. Sam told him what actually happened, but he left that little talk with the distinct impression that he'd never go back to the Pro Bowl. He may not. He had a slight injury, and long after it was healed they were using that injury as an excuse to make him a message carrier, running in plays. He complained that it was tiring, that he couldn't do his best under those conditions, but they let him go right on doing it for almost the whole season. It took him almost a whole year to win back his job as starting tackle. That's why you'll sometimes hear Sam say that the worst thing that ever happened to him was making the 1966 Pro-Bowl squad."

Not that the situation is bright and beautiful for Sam Silas now that he has regained his post as first-string tackle. Certain players and coaches still call him "dumb." His mistakes, no matter how few, are always the subject of long exegeses, and in a 1967 game at Cleveland his old sponsor Chuck Drulis called him a name that is usually restricted to army posts and the hemp mills of certain maximum-security prisons. According to ear-witnesses, the coach shouted the word right in front of one of the highest-ranking members of the Cardinal management. Sam Silas, B.S., M.S., held his temper. "My, my," he said to a friend later. "It certainly is getting permissive around here."

The troubles of Sam Silas and his black teammates finally burst into the open. Late in the season, when the Cardinals were floundering around and doing nothing right, one of the team's black leaders summoned his fellows to a secret meeting in Roy Shivers' apartment on Lindell Boulevard. "Later they tried to say that it was just the taxi-squad Negroes that called the meeting," says Shivers, "but it was called by a regular, and everybody was there. We all felt exactly the same: that it was a shame a ball club with this kind of personnel should be having a hell of a time winning."

Says Prentice Gautt: "It has been said that we were mad, we were bitter. We were not. But we didn't like losing, and we Negroes sat down and said, 'Why are we

216

losing? Let's get together and talk about it.' We could have lived with our grievances, but we wanted to get them out in the open because it would help make us a better unit if some of these things were corrected."

There were impassioned speeches at the three-and-a-half-hour meeting. Veteran Ernie McMillan said: "We should have a common goal: Winning. But if we don't respect each other, hell, forget it! It's a two-way street. Everybody's got to bend a little But we can't do *all* the bending. We're willing to bend, but how far do we have to bend? They want me to be a man out on that football field, but a weakling off it. You can't live two lives. You got to be a man all the time."

Fred Heron said he was only 23 years old, but he understood that many of the Cardinal players were from the South. "They've been raised in the doctrine that a Negro is less than a man because of the color of his skin," he said. "So I'll try to understand that. And I'll just try to say, 'Look, we're on the same team, and you don't *have* to like me, you don't *have* to dig me; I'm not trying to marry your daughter; I don't want to go to bed with your wife. *All I want to do is get into the playoffs!*"

Every Negro at the meeting spoke, and there was unanimity. A list of grievances was drawn up for Coach Winner. According to the men who wrote the statement, it specifically charged Drulis with setting a tone of discrimination on the team and it specifically exempted Winner from the blame, because he was only in his second year as head coach. On the Tuesday before the last game of the season, the list was presented to Winner.

Nothing so juicy could be kept out of the papers, and not many weeks passed before the story made its public appearance. It was batted about in the two major St.

Louis papers for three or four days. The first reaction of the Cardinal front office to the publicity was that the whole affair had been overplayed. It had, in fact, been severely underplayed, but the combination of front-office propaganda and a cooperative local press gradually created the impression that there had been nothing more than a colossal misunderstanding. "This thing is straightened out," said Coach Winner at a time when hardly a step had been taken to do anything except hush matters up. "We do not have a problem here. And we haven't had any more problems here in the past than the majority of the other ball clubs in the NFL. The only difference is that ours got into the papers, and *bang!* we're the ones that got the black eye all over the country." White players were quoted similarly.

From Cardinal co-owner Bill Bidwill and his brother Stormy came statements aimed at showing that the whole matter had been distorted and twisted, which led the thoughtful Homer Floyd, civil-rights worker and one of the better running backs in Big Eight history, to issue a blast: "The reaction of the Cardinal management was instinctive and tragically wrong. The reaction was to defend and justify what had been going on and to attempt to suppress the protests by the Negroes. The result was to confirm the Negro in his belief that racism is institutionalized in the United States. The Cardinal management should have moved quickly to try to correct whatever was bothering the Negro players. Whether the feelings of the Negroes were completely justified was not the main point. The main point was that the Negroes *did* feel that way and what people feel becomes reality for them. Instead of acting, the Cardinal front office belittled the protests, white players sprang up to the defense of the management and you wound up with two camps on the team. In such a situation, it is impossible to maintain an atmosphere of mutual trust between blacks and whites."

When co-owner Bill Bidwill was asked if Chuck Drulis was a prejudiced man, he answered with a straight face, "It was all a misunderstanding about Drulis. We talked to him about it and actually found out that just the opposite was true. In three cases there are Negro players on this team today only because this one coach stood up in meetings and fought for them. They were ready to be cut, and he thought they had a future and fought for them." Another front-office spokesman said that it was impossible that Drulis could have been prejudiced. "Why, once, he went right into a St. Louis tenement to recruit one of our Negro players."

"After a few days of this kind of balderdash," says a white member of the Cardinals, "everybody seemed satisfied, including the newspapers. It was a matter of community pride: the main thing was that the team should win games, not that the Negroes' complaints should get a real hearing. And of course it was accepted that Drulis and the other coaches had no prejudices at all. Didn't they go to tenements to recruit? Didn't they fight to keep their favorite Negroes on the squad? These are standard defenses against charges of racism and they don't mean a thing. The test isn't whether the coach fights to keep a Negro on the squad, but whether he treats a Negro like a man, like an individual, *after* he fights for him. What's so special about fighting to keep a potential star on the team? Is it a sign of fairness to extend to Negroes a right that is automatically extended to whites?"

219

But as the tumult died beneath the efforts to smooth the Cardinals' ruffled public image, the upheaval turned out to have a dramatic and positive effect on the team after all: the eyes of Chuck Drulis were opened, and head coach Charley Winner laid down some tough new policies aimed at cooling off his racist players. Drulis went to the Negro players on the team one by one and apologized. "I'll say this about Coach Drulis," Sam Silas said later. "When he read our grievance letter, he made me very proud to know him. At first I thought he was looking for blood, but he wasn't. He was very pleasant, humble, concerned. I respect the man for that."

Said Bobby Williams: "Coach Drulis told me he didn't have any idea he was doing anything like what we said and if he did he was sorry. He said he didn't know he had been coaching that way. He said if he thought he was really doing that, he'd quit coaching."

Said Willis Crenshaw: "He may not have even known what he was doing. After all, he didn't go around calling people 'nigger' or 'black boy.' He may just have thought he was treating the Negroes in the usual way. He may have been treating Negroes like this for so long that it became a habit. But now that we've let him know about it, we think he'll change. He's changed already."

Drulis himself looked dazed, like a man leaving the scene of an accident. Over and over he would tell anyone who would listen that the furthest thing from his mind had been to treat Negroes and whites differently. He acted genuinely puzzled, genuinely contrite. "I'm not sure what to do now, but whatever it takes, I'll do it," he said. "All I want to do is the right thing. Coach **220** Winner told me not to change my style of coaching, and I can't, anyway. But it *does* give you problems. You have to think twice about hollering at people. Certain coaches can get away with it. Once you have a winner, like Lombardi at Green Bay, you can call your players anything you want. But our trouble started when we tied a game and lost a game that we shouldn't. If we had won another game or two and been in the playoffs, there wouldn't have been a word said. Lombardi calls his players lots of things, but they win. Let them *lose* a few games and see what happens."

Though Charley Winner's first reaction was to help sweep the dirt under the rug, he soon began seeking genuine solutions to the black grievances. The quiet little coach from New Jersey began astonishing the team with blunt talk about the rights of human beings, black *and* white. "Go right ahead and call each other names," he told players of both colors, "but don't let them be racial names, or you'll be playing somewhere else." He honed and polished the words he planned to use in his opening remarks to the team at training camp. "A football team is made of individuals who have a great deal of pride in doing their specific jobs," he wrote. "We have all kinds of nationalities, religions, politics and colors. Our common objective is to win and the only way is to work together, fight together and play together. There's no room for any outside problems on this football team. Our opponents present enough problems without us creating any problems. . . . If someone makes a mistake, it's my job to let him know about it, not you as a player. You'll make mistakes too. No individual is perfect."

Privately, Winner said he would not tolerate any further racial abuse. "If I hear about it, I'll call the player in and talk it over. If he persists after that, I'll get rid of him. Exactly the same is true of coaches." As a joke Winner suggested a staffer go out and buy eight "black power" medallions, one for each member of the coaching staff, and suggested that they wear them on the first day of training camp "to try to relax things a little." More than a gesture is the plan to establish a committee of six players to serve as a buffer and an appeal group in discipline matters between the coaches and the players. And there has been a shakeup of Cardinal personnel. The Negroes have admired Winner's effort, but they feel it will take time to measure the full effect. "A lot of people are prejudiced," said Willis Crenshaw, "on and off this ball club. We don't expect them to change how they feel. They're too old to change. But we want them to curtail it when it hurts the ball club. That's all we ask."

Said Bobby Williams: "It's not that we want them to love us, but they can smooth things out a lot. It's not up to the Negroes, it's up to the whites. We're doing the best we can. We ask them not to treat us like little Greek gods, but just like people, flesh and blood people like them."

"We'll wait and see," said the respected Ernie McMillan, who serves on the park board in his own St. Louis suburb. "But it's important that everybody understands the issues. It isn't only that the St. Louis Cardinals lost a few ball games because of race prejudice. That's not the big loss. The big loss is this: we Negro players are automatic heroes in the Negro community, if only because we've got a certain amount of fame. People look up to us, turn to us for advice. We could be going back to the Negro community and telling them *not* to burn, *not* to riot, *not* to cause trouble.

But what kind of hypocrites would we be to go back and tell the Negroes that a better day is coming, when that day isn't even in sight yet on the playing field?"

Prentice Gautt, who has crossed into the white world of collegiate coaching, agrees with his old teammates. "It's a sad thing to face, but racial prejudice is almost a tradition in sports," Coach Gautt says. "Some people just have to be able to look down on other people, and they give the Negro the feeling that no matter what he does he will never be an equal. The long-range problems will take a long time to solve. But if they can't be solved in sports, where can they be solved? Sports has been following when it's supposed to lead. The change should start today. Not tomorrow. *Today.*"

x

PRODUCTION STAFF FOR TIME INCORPORATED

John L. Hallenbeck (Vice President and Director of Production),
Robert E. Foy and Caroline Ferri
Text photocomposed under the direction of Albert J. Dunn and Arthur J. Dunn